ROUTLEDGE LIBRARY EDITIONS: LIBRARY AND INFORMATION SCIENCE

Volume 95

SEX MAGAZINES IN THE LIBRARY COLLECTION

SEX MAGAZINES IN THE LIBRARY COLLECTION
A Scholarly Study of Sex in Serials and Periodicals

Edited by
PETER GELLATLY

Routledge
Taylor & Francis Group
LONDON AND NEW YORK

First published in 1981 by The Haworth Press, Inc.

This edition first published in 2020
by Routledge
2 Park Square, Milton Park, Abingdon, Oxon OX14 4RN

and by Routledge
52 Vanderbilt Avenue, New York, NY 10017

Routledge is an imprint of the Taylor & Francis Group, an informa business

© 1981 The Haworth Press, Inc.

All rights reserved. No part of this book may be reprinted or reproduced or utilised in any form or by any electronic, mechanical, or other means, now known or hereafter invented, including photocopying and recording, or in any information storage or retrieval system, without permission in writing from the publishers.

Trademark notice: Product or corporate names may be trademarks or registered trademarks, and are used only for identification and explanation without intent to infringe.

British Library Cataloguing in Publication Data
A catalogue record for this book is available from the British Library

ISBN: 978-0-367-34616-4 (Set)
ISBN: 978-0-429-34352-0 (Set) (ebk)
ISBN: 978-0-367-41792-5 (Volume 95) (hbk)
ISBN: 978-0-367-41803-8 (Volume 95) (pbk)
ISBN: 978-0-367-81627-8 (Volume 95) (ebk)

Publisher's Note
The publisher has gone to great lengths to ensure the quality of this reprint but points out that some imperfections in the original copies may be apparent.

Disclaimer
The publisher has made every effort to trace copyright holders and would welcome correspondence from those they have been unable to trace.

Sex Magazines In The Library Collection

A Scholarly Study of Sex in Serials and Periodicals

Edited with an Introduction by
PETER GELLATLY

A Monographic Supplement to The Serials Librarian
(Volume 4, 1979/1980)

THE HAWORTH PRESS
New York

©1981 by The Haworth Press, Inc. All rights reserved. No part of this work may be reproduced or utilized in any form or by any means, electronic or mechanical, including photocopying, microfilm and recording, or by any information storage and retrieval system, without permission in writing from the publisher.

The Haworth Press, 149 Fifth Avenue, New York, New York 10010

Library of Congress Cataloging in Publication Data
Main entry under title:

Sex magazines in the library collection.

   Includes bibliographical references and index.
   1. Libraries--Special collections--Sex oriented periodicals--Addresses, essays, lectures. I. Gellatly, Peter. II. Serials librarian.
Z688.E76S49   026'.3067   80-15011
ISBN 0-917724-16-X

Printed in the United States of America

Sex Magazines In The Library Collection
A Scholarly Study of Sex in Serials and Periodicals

A Monographic Supplement to
The Serials Librarian, *Volume 4 (1979/1980)*

INTRODUCTION
Sex Magazines in the Library Collection   1
    Peter Gellatly

Prolegomena to Pornography in Greek and Roman Antiquity   9
    Lawrence S. Thompson

    This is a brief survey of literary and pictorial treatment of sexuality in classical antiquity, with some reference to comparable situations in modern times. The nature, motivation, and effect of sexual themes in ancient literature and art are reviewed. It is pointed out that the best writers and artists of antiquity treated sexual themes with delicacy and sensitivity acceptable to any reasonable person. There were scruffy and scataological treatments of sexual themes in antiquity not much different from those of our time.

WORTH REPEATING: ARTICLES OF INTEREST FROM THE NON-LIBRARY PRESS
Sex Magazines   17
    J. J. Gayford

    This article presents an analysis and discussion of 72 British sex magazines. About 10% had a strong sado-masochistic content and tended to be more expensive. Twenty-five percent give no indication that they were not for sale to minors. The majority were published in London or Surrey, with 35% claiming a female editor. Over half invited reader participation with letters, and nine had professional advisors. Nearly one-fifth had contact advertisements. Some magazines tried to present a respectable front with a title, or sub-title, which conveyed the impression of a serious scientific publication.

Sex Magazines: Problems of Acquisition, Retention, Display, and Defense in Public and Academic Libraries   27
    Bruce A. Shuman
    Karen Dalziel Tallman

    This article is an in-depth examination of the problems encountered by public and academic libraries seeking to acquire, maintain, and make available sex magazines, a term not readily definable. Indexing is stressed as the first justification for retention, and typical tactics of challenge and some appropriate library responses are explored. The article includes original "scorecards" for the determination of the likely controversiality of a title, and concludes with a few scenarios of the future, which establish that the problems now confronting libraries, insofar as these titles are concerned, are temporary, and will, for one reason or another, not be with us in 20 years.

Treatment of Sexually Oriented Magazines by Libraries   47
Roy M. Mersky
Michael L. Richmond

Assuming obscene or scatalogical material to be appropriate for inclusion in a library collection, this article discusses the fact that simply obtaining serial material of this nature poses problems from the ordering to the payment. With the proliferation of new material, selection of appropriate additions also proves difficult for the librarian building such a collection. Once the threshold problems of getting the material into the building have been surmounted, cataloging, binding, and preservation add to them. Having acquired and treated this material, the librarian must take into account laws prohibiting its dissemination for other than scientific or research purposes. Thus, the collection must reside in an area accessible only by special permission. Further, the librarian must maintain a firm stand where the needs of the collection dictate acquisition of this material; he or she must stand fast against the wrath of self-appointed censors and sanctimonious blue-nosed members of boards and governing panels, maintaining the tradition of the profession forwarding free access to information.

Sex, Serials and the Law   53
Richard C. Dahl

In this article, the problem of sex, serials and the law is seen as one that can be summed up by the word "change." Changing statutes, court decisions, technology, and attitudes make this area of law one of uncertainty. Unfortunately, the state of the law is further muddled by the fact that there are almost as many dumb cases and dreadful laws as there are dirty books and disgusting pictures. This happy situation is not improved by looking to inconsistent cases that only increase the complexity of a tough problem.

Erotic Magazines and the Law   57
Jerold Nelson

Censorship incidents involving erotic magazines which were cited in the *Newsletter on Intellectual Freedom* between July 1973 and November 1978 are analyzed in this article to assess the impact of the Supreme Court's Miller decisions. The high frequency of incidents suggests that there has been some effect, but there is not sufficient information available to arrive at precise conclusions. Data concerning the chronological and geographical distribution are reported.

Children's Rights in the Library: A Personal View 63
Cynthia R. Howe

Exploring the problem of children's rights regarding sexual literature in the public library requires discussion of the following: a definition of the public library's role in the community; the nature of the literature; a definition of the age categories and the subject matter associated with each category; the library's role in the selection and accessibility of sexual literature to minors; and the parent's role in introducing the child to such materials. In this article the author discusses the problems as seen through the eyes of a parent, and gives her opinions for possible solutions.

INTO THE HOPPER: GOVERNMENT SERIALS
Sex Themes in Federal Serials 69
Joe Morehead

An examination of over 50 federal government periodicals and annuals reveals a wide diversity of concerns of government agencies. From agriculture to zoology, sexual subjects are treated. As this paper indicates, articles in the journals range from highly technical to popular. Of particular importance in the last decade has been the subject of sex discrimination. The Serial Set is examined for its coverage in House and Senate reports of obscenity and pornography.

Sexology: A Personal Guide to the Serial Literature 75
Barrett W. Elcano
Vern Bullough

The authors present a historical survey, chronologically detailing the origin and development of selected, scholarly serials devoted to the dissemination of research studies dealing with sexology and sex-related research topics. Prior to the Second World War, coverage of sex research was confined primarily to non-English language serial publications and the article reflects this early emphasis. Since the Second World War, the article focuses on increasingly available English language serials in sex research. User access through traditional serial indexing sources is discussed. The article concludes with a selected bibliography of current serials in sexology, listing serials in sex research, birth control, homosexuality, and transvestism and effeminism.

A Select Annotated Bibliography of Gay and Lesbian Periodicals 87
Frederick McEnroe

This annotated bibliography of 32 items represents a selection of American, Canadian, and overseas magazines, newspapers, and newsletters currently published by a variety of gay and lesbian organizations and associations. Included in the article is a short historical introduction to the homosexual civil rights and gay liberation movements in Europe and the United States, with mention of some historically important periodicals. The article closes with a short unannotated list of periodicals which could not be examined by the compiler, and with a list of publications devoted to gay male erotica.

If There Were a *Sex Index* **...** 99
Sanford Berman

An index to sex-related periodicals is proposed and a model provided in this article. Standard vocabularies are found to be too limited, "clinical," and judgmental.

Contributors 137

Index 139

INTRODUCTION

SEX MAGAZINES IN THE LIBRARY COLLECTION

When Sally Rand died a year or so ago, the *Vancouver Sun* published the following tribute to her:

She worked almost to the end. She died the other day aged 75. And now it can be said. The bluestockings were right. Miss Rand did excite passions and stimulate hot thoughts. And she did it all with illusion. She put sex in the head, where it is terribly subversive. This quite escapes the clumsy skin-merchants of our own let-it-all-hang-out age, who should be indicted not for making sex corrupting, but making it tedious. It gives a certain cackling delight to think that an old woman in her 70s was more sensual than all the bare naked bods that hang from the meat-hooks of our magazine counters.[1]

Thus did a daily newspaper venerate the memory of an unique performer and at the same time rebuke the too literal decadence of the present day.

Sex magazines do, of course, expose with some frankness the seamy maunderings of the minds that produce them; and if the present crop gives offense, the offense is really not any more gross than it has ever been. What is new is that the under-the-counter trade in such magazines has been replaced by a booming trade conducted in the open and more or less sanctioned·by everybody's board of trade. Full disclosure, a shibboleth of the age, attains new meaning in this particular area.

Growth in the number of sex magazines parallels and outstrips that of the general rate of publishing; and if the one is phenomenal, the other taxes belief. There have always been scholarly magazines devoted to the study of sex, of course; and although these become fairly abundant, their number is not great. The popular variety of the species is now, however, plainly ubiquitous. And this uniquity gives rise to problems of various sorts.

Every drugstore in the country has *Playboy* and *Penthouse* for sale, and every Main Street, in even small places, has its "adult" bookstore. Even the most liberal-minded come to feel annoyance over the plethora of garish and tasteless—not to say offensive—magazines that thrust their way into the public view. And while most of us give ready assent to the notion of First Amendment freedoms, there is a feeling, not hard to substantiate, that the Amendment's intent is being bent out of shape by some fairly rank commercialism on the part of the publishers of these magazines. It is no surprise to find that constant review of the First

Amendment is taking place in order to establish as precisely as possible what its limits are, both in this area and others. One can assume that the process will never resolve itself satisfactorily, and this is perhaps as it should be. Moreover, the freedom of speech/censorship debate, which is essentially a First Amendment debate, exercises in its own way a restraint upon excesses in either direction, since these in general constitute an affront both to decency and common-sense.

Still, there is no denying that the question of press censorship is a worrying one. And nowhere is it debated more hotly than in the area of the popular sex magazine. Here the debate is voluble and not without acrimony. It has led, in extreme cases, which sadly exist even now, to the imprisonment of such as Ginzburg of *Eros* fame and the indictment on criminal charges of others like Larry Flynt of *Hustler*. Ginzburg, whose publication pales beside many latter-day examples of the genre, went to prison for having sent pornographic material (specifically, an ad depicting an 18th century couple engaged in what was then referred to as country matters) through the U.S. mails. Very pale stuff indeed beside the leering salaciousness that confronts one nowadays on most magazine racks. The Flynt matter was more serious; it is now before the appeal courts.

It is necessary, in speaking of sex magazines, to define the terms "pornography" and "obscenity." And this task is laborious and not altogether productive.

Definitions of the latter term have been put forward endlessly. The best still remains Justice Potter Stewart's: "I can't define it, but I know it when I see it." Yet the difficulty in accepting so loose a definition, as well as its beauty, perhaps, is that then everybody becomes his or her own judge of what is obscene and what is not. This would be fine if the millenium were here, but, as things are, concessions must be made to current standards and fashions. Under such an interpretation, reason and proportion are obviously sacrificed to expediency. For example, it is not unheard of even now for persons engaged in the promotion of outrageous smut to claim merit for their product, and one might expect such activity to intensify in the absence of more stringent requirements as to what is and is not acceptable.

On the other hand, it has to be admitted that a tightening-up of the definition results in difficulties of even wider consequence. At its most extreme point, of course, such action opens the door to censorship and all its attendant complications and ills.

If one were to attempt to distinguish between the terms "pornography" and "obscenity," one would soon find oneself bogged down hopelessly in semantic and legalistic confusions. Both terms conjure up various forms of unpleasantness and even of pathology. The first, however, is generally held to be of more amiable and less deleterious content than is the other—presumably one can be amused by pornography, but never by obscenity. It is hard to find what is called redeeming social value in either, however, and attempts to do so are pretty generally consigned to frustration. There are exceptions, as some works described as pornographic can also be great works of art (such obvious examples come to mind as *Lady Chatterley* and Joyce's *Ulysses*). "Hard core" pornography must, of course, seek its justification in some other way, as at the end of the scale it occupies artistic merit is not generally in the purview of either supplier or customer.

All of these matters are mulled over interminably by librarians and others, and the consensus seems to be that no consensus is possible. It can be readily assumed, however, that discussion of them will continue; and it is in this that hope appears of some eventual conciliation in the embattled area of the sex magazine.

Certain works considered pornographic, or at least admitting of the possibility, are undeniably works of literary merit. Yet in suggesting the worth of such works as *Lolita*, the *Tropics* of Henry Miller, or *Memoirs of a Woman of Pleasure*, among many others, is to prompt an immediate chorus of objection even now, when it might be expected that old works of acclaim, regardless of past doubts, would be accorded general acceptance. The perniciousness of such works, while denied by people of ordinary fastidiousness and aplomb, leads others to deplore them as irredeemably banal and offensive. Strictures of the sort aside, however, one has to admit that not everybody is a likely reader for works containing sexual references, regardless of the way in which these are presented.

It is an unfortunate propensity of human nature that while nobody is obliged to read something he or she would rather not, many of those who choose against participating themselves are eager to deny others the right to decide for themselves what they want to do. The unfairness of this position, while blatant enough, eludes its proponents, who feel justified, for whatever reason, in attempting to give their own personal rules a community-wide application.

Community standards are, of course, elusive and hard to define—they are protean and subject to continual revision. Once, for instance, Petty and Gibson girls were objects of prurient interest, whereas now even the air-brushed and uxorious "playmate of the month" scarcely merits a second glance. Social attitudes are, of course, seldom, if ever, free of pose, and authors like Frank Harris and Henry Miller and others whose works have been banned have always had their admirers, as, for that matter, have artists like Beardsley and Schiele, whose uncompromising depiction of the human body, although of consummate artistry, once caused wholesale consternation.

It is true, nevertheless, that a taste for the unconventional and titillating slices its way back through history to the time of Plato and Apuleius, and no doubt beyond that to the caves of our remotest ancestors. Pornography, like music, is a constant of all times and places.

It is only comparatively recently that sex has become a subject of serious study. An Engish author recounts in a recent book how he enjoyed as a boy reading the medical books in his father's library, and how he was particularly taken by the anatomical illustrations in them. Even now it is possible to assume that Havelock Ellis is proving instructive to young library users, although certainly much more inflammatory material is available nearby. And, it must be added, material that is assuredly less firm in its science and vocabulary.

Joseph Brodsky, in speaking of his ideal town, says:

I'd want a libary there, and in its empty halls I'd browse through books containing precisely the same number of commas as the dirty words in daily gutter language— words that haven't yet broken into literary prose. Much less into verse.[2]

There are not too many libraries nowadays that can claim empty halls (surely an unenviable condition at any time), and it is likely, too, that the gutter language Brodsky speaks of can be found in fair supply on almost any library shelf. The use of demotic speech is now almost mandatory in works of fiction; and while this by no means assures literary success, it is all the same commonplace. The fact is that most people use one form of speech in conversation and another in writing; and the distinction maintains itself, even though it tends to blur as time proceeds (it remains, of course, in scientific writing, where what would be considered stilted and even foolish in a piece of creative writing may be needed for preciseness and clarity). Our language does become less inhibited, Edwin Newman and relative crowds of purists notwithstanding, and who is to say that this is not a good thing?

In any event, language itself is the target of many a would-be censor, as librarians know full well. They know, too, that the censor has followed close on the heels of the artist in all ages, not least our own. It is, of course, possible to oppose repressive measures without approving of permissiveness. But to object to permissiveness poses dangers of its own, as Peter Ustinov, the author who found illumination in his father's medical books, suggests:

However people may carp or cavil about what has become known as the Permissive Age, I believe that free communication, even if pushed to excess, is infinitely preferable to the murk of ignorance. Better a generation that has come to terms with its physical existence than one in which a lack of knowledge is veiled by social propriety and the hypocritical grace notes of piety and breeding. Even pornography, which is the antithesis of the erotic, and which has now settled on us as a garish consumer-oriented commodity, is, in its early stages, a liberator from the greater evil of social censorship.

It may seem strange that I can write with evident feeling of a battle which today is won. I do so only to remind the incredulous that it was not always so; that

. . . up to relatively recently there were prejudices, both parental and institutional, which made subjects of vital interest to human happiness taboo.[3]

Ustinov's cheerful assertion that the battle is won is surprising, though of course great gains have been made in recent years in the frank and open exchange of views on subjects until now considered, as he puts it, taboo.

If adult susceptibilities are affronted by much newsstand material, the effect such material has upon children is bound to be a matter of concern. It is not possible to accept with confidence the notion that as children grow up quickly nowadays, they no longer need the sort of sheltering that was accorded previous generations. The prurience of such publications as *Playboy* and *Penthouse* may not constitute a worry for the adult population at large, but can scarcely be thought proper fare for children. And it is the fact of ready access to these and other perhaps less amiable publications that is disturbing to parents. These, of course, are not alone in feeling that the situation bears scrutiny.

The feeling persists that what is at stake is less a concern for freedom, intellectual or otherwise, than the right of publishers and distributors to make a profit. It is wrong, of course, to say that the activities of these people are carried out at the expense of children, but parents at least can be excused for suspecting that children's rights tend to be obscured in the scramble for profits. And if efforts to control the offending publications are themselves crass and offensive, neither the blatancy of the publications nor their unsuitability for a general audience, one containing children, can be denied.

One hesitates to call upon the specter of D. H. Lawrence, who has been praised, with conspicuous inappropriateness, as the progenitor of the modern sexual revolution. The fact is that Lawrence was repulsed by coarseness and promiscuity, and would surely have considered the routine sexual freedom touted by the Heffners and Gucciones of our time as perverse and destructive. He held that the highest virtues do not change, and that these encompass notions of sobriety and faithfulness. He was in fact a Puritan, but without the Puritan's insistence upon form and ritual. It is arguable that Lawrence was in his way as intractable and demanding as any enthusiast for a cause, but this is beside the point. What is germane is that Lawrence had a dread of anything that was demeaning or could "tarnish." And certainly, in his canon, the sort of sex purveyed by the common newsstand magazine would have fit into this category. One can scarcely blame those who find the present situation trying, no matter how they regard Lawrence and his theories.

It is difficult to assess the damage that sex magazines do, although there is a general awareness, almost visceral in its strength, that they are in fact damaging. One tends to discount tales of hideous crimes committed by youngsters or others with insalubrious reading habits. Nevertheless, such tales continue to circulate, and they are, to say the least, chilling. About all that can be done under the circumstances is to hold tight to reason, confident in the belief that the world, which has always had crime, is likely to hold together, and is no worse in this respect than it has ever been.

One reads of court battles in which librarians find themselves having to defend books held to be unsuitable for general consumption because of their sexual content or the manner in which this is expressed. The charges arise generally out of what is described as a concerned effort to keep the offending items off library shelves. In instances of the sort, the librarian is hard put to muster an appropriate defense, as often the publication in question has little enough to recommend it. Battles over such works as *Lady Chatterley's Lover* and the *Catcher in the Rye*, one likes to think, are in the past, even if they must be refought from time to time to satisfy some local need. What is common now is for the librarian to have to defend the right to keep a particular item on the shelf, regardless of the merits of the item itself. In other words, the issue is fought on principle rather than on the merits, real or imagined, of the item. There is unquestionably point in this. There is also the painful realization that good people can be hurt in such confrontations. It is one thing to fight a battle in which, say, the fate of Joyce's *Ulysses* is contested, and quite another to do battle on behalf of a scruffy little item that somebody feels for whatever reason (most likely the item's very scruffiness) ought to be banished from the library. Even victory in such an instance has to seem murky.

Persons who undertake to attack libraries assert time and again, as one did recently on the *Donahue* television show, that every act of selection is also an act of censorship in that, as budgets are not unlimited, the selecting of one item requires the rejecting of another. This assessment of what goes into the selection process is not entirely accurate, but it does serve to underline the caveat that the librarian's judgment can be called into question by the community he or she serves. This does in fact happen, and with startling frequency.

One gets the impression in examining court testimony that the defense mounted by the librarian in such cases is often meager. The reason for this is apparent—the works being defended are themselves so meager that there is not much to be said for them. Matters are further complicated by the almost inevitable intrusion into the proceedings of external issues. And in this deeply held convictions can be flouted, and personal assumptions put to the challenge. It is rarely possible, for instance, to convince a person bent upon expunging a book from a library collection that his reasons for wanting this are not universally convincing. One can only admire the courage with which libraries respond to such challenges. If, as is generally acknowledged, repressive measures are abhorrent, so certainly is censorship, whatever the guise in which it presents itself.

The idea that sex magazines have a place in the library makes itself felt. Few librarians, however, are willing to invest more than a token amount in them. As suggested, accountability makes most shy away from the thought of having to defend a purchase capable of arousing antagonism in their clients. This is not to suggest that librarians lack the courage of their convictions, but rather to indicate that they know how few sex magazines have a content that makes them worth having. They are well aware, too, of the need for an evenhanded allocation of funds among the various areas of the library's interest, and that injudicious spending in one creates problems in another. Finally, they have to contend with that intangible quantity—how they feel themselves about the publications they order. In choosing there is always an element of subjectivity; and clearly there will be hesitation in the ordering of an item the librarian finds disagreeable or repugnant. Again, however, a qualification must be added, as it is not to be supposed that librarians are incapable of rising above personal tastes and prejudices in a matter of the sort. The fact is that they order, within the means at their disposal, whatever publications are needed to carry out the library's program.

Most libraries do in fact stock at least a representative handful of sex magazines. It is an unusual library that does not subscribe nowadays to such relatively bland publications as *Playboy* and *Penthouse;* and most of any size have on their shelves items of a considerably more exceptional nature than these.

Ervin Gaines, once chairperson of the American Library Association's Intellectual Freedom Committee, is quoted by Helen Colton, an editor of *Forum,* to the effect that pornographic publications, including presumably sex magazines, fulfill a social need of unknown dimensions. "Pornography," he says, "must be important or it wouldn't be so prevalent. It has some meaning in our lives that we do not understand." And he goes on to suggest that it is necessary for the benefit of future scholars and researchers that libraries collect it.[4] Colton herself indicates that libraries are making an effort to see that this is done. She says that the largest collection of pornography in the world is to be found in the Vatican Library, and that other significant collections exist. She gives as an example the library of the University of California at Fullerton.[5]

Apart from the rife and usually rancorous misunderstandings that the presence of sex magazines on the shelf gives rise to, the librarian encounters other difficulties in dealing with these publications. One is in knowing what sort of cataloging and indexing to accord them. It has been pointed out by Berman and others that present methods of doing this fail to make sufficient allowance for the frequently divergent views expressed in such publications. This objection is countered by the suggestion that if there is sufficient latitude in existing schemes to take account of the atom bomb, there ought to be enough for a categorizing of sex and its components. The alternative viewpoint is not, however, to be put down so lightly; and changes in cataloging and indexing forms are constantly being urged upon the authorities at the Library of Congress and elsewhere. It cannot be supposed, of course, that these authorities are insensitive to real need. Changes are being made, and some of far-reaching consequence.

The attitude is fortunately gone that once led a research library to accord a work on the *Folies Bergères* an author entry alone, omitting other possibilities, because the cataloger was offended by some of the book's illustrations. Librarians have long since transcended the feeling that they are keepers of the community's morals. They can be excused some skepticism, however, regarding the level of morality displayed by library customers who check out copies of sex magazines without benefit of the circulation desk or who razor out of them items to which they wish to give attention away from library premises.

For all this, librarians recognize their social responsibility to provide the public with the material it wants to read; and if the choice the public makes seems sometimes of dubious merit, this is a hazard that librarians accept.

Peter Gellatly

REFERENCES

1. "From Her Fans Everywhere," *Vancouver Sun,* September 1, 1979, p. A4.
2. Joseph Brodsky, "Plato Elaborated," *New Yorker,* March 12, 1979, p. 40.
3. Peter Ustinov, *Dear Me* (Harmondsworth, Eng.: Penguin, 1977), p. 125.
4. Helen Colton, "Update on Pornography," *Humanist* 38, no. 6 (Nov./Dec. 1978): 48.
5. Colton, p. 48.

PROLEGOMENA TO PORNOGRAPHY IN GREEK AND ROMAN ANTIQUITY

Lawrence S. Thompson

In general the ancients had a wholesome attitude toward sexual functions and the human body. To be sure, some Athenians raised half an eyebrow about Spartan youth of both sexes exercising together in the nude, and a few remaining old line Republican Romans felt that Ovid's *Ars amatoria* might just as well have never been put on papyrus. While the Greeks recognized homosexuality as one way of life, there was a general disapproval of the coarse and mawkish poems of Straton of Sardis (fl. A.D. 125) on homosexual love, preserved in the *Antologia palatina*. The customary Greek attitudes are best expressed in the famous inscription at Delphi, "Nothing in excess."

There have always been and always will be those who revel in gossip about the sexual habits of others, and it is often an amusing pastime when no malice is involved. But it is difficult to forgive the snickering Alexandrians who read tribadism into the poems of Sappho of Lesbos, a talented lady completely devoted to some of her equally talented pupils. George Lyman Kittredge was once quoted, "If there was anything reprehensible about Sappho's dedication to her pupils, you might as well arraign me for zoophily for my love for my dog." My notion about Sappho is that she made her biggest mistake in her unhappy passion for Phaon in middle age.

There is no question but that ancient erotic traditions have been reflected in modern times, but there has been no systematic research, to my knowledge, on the direct influence. One can find all sorts of parallels between sexuality in ancient and modern literature, for that matter, between occidental and oriental, Islamic and Christian, and so on. Thumb through Thompson's *Motif Index* for abundant evidence. Yet the enduring attraction of all aspects of antiquity appears frequently in modern erotic and quasi-erotic humor. Take some of the centaur cartoons in *The New Yorker*. One of them shows two of the fabled semi-anthropomorphic creatures chatting with a worried look: "We may be the last of our kind. They've passed some pretty tough sodomy laws in this state." Or the same pair, in a scholarly stance, inspecting a brood mare on a Blue Grass farm: "You know, that proves that even nature can make mistakes."

About 1974 there was a delightfully imaginative show at a hole-in-the-wall theater near the Pantheon in Paris entitled *L'Histoire du thêâtre*. The first of the six scenes (the last a parody of *A Streetcar Named Desire*) was a pantomimic version of the origin of the Greek comedy. A couple of nude girls, equipped with enormous phalloi that would have done credit to the Titans, cavorted around the stage amidst rustic revelry. Some of the sexual traditions of ancient civilization are amusing and even instructive to us; but we are likely to look on these aspects of antiquity as antiquarians and scholars, not as writers or artists taking direct inspiration.

Perhaps antiquity acquired a special reputation for erotic wickedness from the bluenoses, from the publishers of the Delphine editions through the schoolmasters up to the time when Greek and Latin came to be considered obsolete in most secondary schools (save the better private institutions). The notion that ancients were naughty as a matter of accepted custom was undoubtedly perpetuated by the editors of school texts. There is an amusing passage in Horace's "Trip to Brundisium" (*Sermones*, I, v, 82-86) in which the balding, middle-aged dean of Roman letters tried to extract a commitment from a B-girl to join him in his room in a flea-ridden provincial inn after the tavern closed. She was a no-show. The first two lines are in high wit, the second two in bad taste, one of the few such passages in Horace. But the second two were bowdlerized in the text my students were using (I was using a Teubner text), and there was a near conflict with an earnest young man who failed to translate the passage expurgated from his text. More ridiculous was the omission, in a school text, of a line from Ovid, "Zeus came unto Danae in a shower of gold" (*Metamorphoses*, IV, 611). And equally confusing in class recitation! Even the Loeb editors are often prone to protect the morals of scholars. The lines from Horace mentioned above are not translated literally, but rather in a decorous phrase leaving no doubts about the situation. And the Greek volumes, most published before the "new freedom," are often dappled with passages in Latin rather than English (there is no such modesty on the part of editors of *Collection "Guillaume Budé"* or the Reclam parallel texts).

We have abundant iconographic evidence of what we, even in the late 20th century, might consider pornography in antiquity. Here is a digression which might better go into our sister journal, *Library and Archival Security*, but it is a valid scholium here. The monumental *Corpus vasorum*, a seemingly impossible dream of scholars that has come true, includes all the vase paintings, not excluding the erotic. It is a fairly expensive set, running well into four figures. A midwestern university had the complete set shelved in the general collection with the separate plates in portfolios. A faculty member learned that some of the plates with erotic scenes were posted with tape on the walls of dormitories, and he protested vigorously about the lack of security for a virtually irreplaceable set, at least in single parts. The library responded inappropriately; rather, a bindery clerk did: the surviving plates, on stiff and partially friable stock, were bound, oversewn and returned to the open shelves. Many of the remaining plates showing lewd satyrs and willing maenads have been brutally ripped from the oversewn bindings and doubtless adorn the walls of every fraternity from Alpha Delta Pi to Zeta Beta Tau. Probably the most serious error was committed by the artists themselves, covering so much of the area in black that the plates don't copy well on electrostatic machines. The late Randolph G. Adams would have taken grim scholarly glee in this episode, had he known of it when he wrote his classic essay on "Librarians as Enemies of Books."

Greek vase painting and a few pieces of sculpture were often erotically humorous and occasionally obviously for titillation. It would be difficult to assume that a megalophallic satyr on a wine jug did not extract a laugh from young Athenian bucks in the local dram shops. On the other hand, scenes of intercourse (including buccal and anal), orgies, and group sex were obviously for the same type of audience to which my fellow Kentuckian, Larry Flynt of Salyersville, appeals in *Hustler*. Unlike the Chinese erotic art, there are relatively few scenes with voyeurs (generally voyeuses in the orient), although there is more sly humor than lubricity in the Chinese representations of erotic scenes, e.g., the *macho* standing at the bottom of a swing while the *hembra* on the seat is pushed towards him by a voyeuse. On the other hand, the Romans of the Empire did not hesitate to show identifiable figures on scandalous cameos and gems, possibly as political satire or even underground art. One gem shows Augustus having intercourse with the wife of Maecenas while the apparently willing cuckold snoozes sitting upright. A cameo ascribed to Artemon of Rhodes shows Livia, incorrigible schemer that she was, offering two nude virgins to Augustus. Another gem shows a pimpish-looking Otho presenting the nude Poppaea to Nero. And Suetonius tells the same stories (to say nothing of his scandalous yarns about Tiberius!).

The Etruscans outdid their teachers, the Greeks, in erotic art, much of it as vivid as that of the ancient Indians. To add further confusion to the vexed question of Etruscan ethnology, one cannot help but wonder whether scenes of different varieties of sexual acrobatics, soixante-neuf, sodomy, and all manner of variants from missionary style might not reflect some possible contact between India and the earliest civilized inhabitants of Tuscany. In any event, some Etruscan art was sufficiently lewd to qualify for the *museo segreto* of the Vatican and even today is not generally available.

The Catholic Italian attitudes towards matters sexual have always been the object of amusement by northern Europeans and North Americans of both major Christian sects. The best example, perhaps, is the situation with the well preserved *lupinaria* in Pompeii, where there are paintings over the cribs in the bordellos showing the specialties of each bawd. There is no mistaking how to get there: in lieu of modern red lights (Christmas tree lights in the Caribbean) there are winged phalloi in mosaic on the sidewalks pointing to the *fornix* (arched entrance to the *lupinaria*, hence fornication). The last time I saw the place was in the late

1930s, with a Danish lady who was a candidate for a degree in ancient art at Copenhagen. A friend in Naples, a third-order Dominican, warned us that the rascally guides would tell us that the Italian government forbade ladies to enter the *lupinaria,* though no such law existed save in the minds of the guides who wanted a *mordida* to violate the imaginary statute. We so informed the guide and entered the *lupinaria* to his great annoyance. But to assuage his feelings I slipped him a five dollar Confederate note, of which I always took a good supply for use in eastern and southern Europe in the '30s. This one is probably still circulating among gullible Neapolitans.

It cannot be too strongly emphasized that the human body, presented for its beauty, has always been one of the major themes of occidental art. Sophocles was thinking primarily of man's mind when he wrote the greatest ode of the tragedies, to man, beginning "Many mysteries there are, none more mysterious than man" (*Antigone,* 330 *et seq.*). But the great tragedian must also have had in the back of his mind the dexterity and beauty of the body of *homo sapiens.* Nudity in the best tradition of Greek art is not offensive to any thoughtful person, hopefully not even to a thoughtful R. C. Neapolitan guide or even an educated Southern Baptist, nay, even to Anita Bryant. The Cnidian Aphrodite (ca. 330 B.C.) in the Vatican Museum and, somewhat further along the line of the erotic, the Callipygian Venus in the National Museum of Naples, were designed to show the sensuous character of the goddess of love; but as far as art is concerned, they are almost chaste in concept and execution. The latter has been reproduced in provocative style on Greek vases and Roman gems, but the original statue is a tribute in stone to the beauty of woman. The ancient statues of Hermaphrodite, even those showing the unusual combination of the *pudenda,* are generally in good taste (e.g., the third century B.C. Hermaphrodite in the Louvre, with the curious addition of a mattress by Bernini), illustrating what is basically a charming legend of the definitive union of two lovers.

Alongside pictorial representation in all media, the theater, even more than other genres of prose and poetry, has always been a favored vehicle of the pornographers. Here both language and image can be reproduced. The scruffy theaters on Times Square and West 42nd have a stronger appeal to the rednecks of Manhattan than do the even scruffier "adult" books in the nearby sleazy stores, for the proletariat does not, cares not to, often cannot, read. Yet a picture is worth a thousand words, both in intellectual and animalistic moods. The Laocoön tells a dramatic story of hybris and retribution that appeals to the thinking man as much as the Etruscan murals titillated *homo animalis.* On another level, one can hardly condemn man for enjoying the dirty joke or harmless earthy drama. The earliest phallic comedy had the same appeal to the good old country boys of Attica and was received in the same spirit as are the robust stories told around the wood stove in the First Brother's filling station in

Plains. The sight of an exaggerated phallos on a prancing satyr in Greek village festivals of the sixth and fifth centuries B.C. amused the Hellenic wool hats as much as the Renaissance intellectual was delighted by the sly humor in Rabelais' catalogue of the fictitious library of St. Victor.

The writers of the old comedy, above all Aristophanes, achieved the ultimate in sophisticated use of sexual themes, only feebly reflected today in *Hair, O! Calcutta,* and similar drama (one suspects successful only because of more attractive presentation of nudity than in the porno flicks). Yes, *Lysistrata* is ribald, but it is ribaldry with a message, presented meaningfully and with consummate art. Lysistrata was a lady who could have worn white gloves in the Old South, and I would have had no hesitation to have had her as chaperone for my daughters at a debutante ball. Aristophanes revealed her as a lady of wit and imagination who could have found her place in any milieu, in the choir of a Cumberland Presbyterian Church if she so chose. A significant aspect of Aristophanes' art is that he could use sexuality, even coarseness, to the great delight of his audiences and for effective social and political satire.

Aristophanes' use of sexual themes involved a skill, a special endowment, that occurs sporadically in literature, especially the dramatic, throughout the ages. Fourteen centuries later the pious but witty Hrotswitha von Gandersheim provided cloistered audiences with a dramatic version of the uproarious tale of the three Christian virgins who foiled the evil designs of Dulcitius on their virtue. Less well known internationally, but of comparable genius, was the late William H. Townsend, Lexington, KY attorney and Lincoln authority, who could tell the raunchiest of Lincoln stories to the Kentucky Civil War Round Table and extract Homeric laughs from the Methodist ministers and local topers alike. His classic pieces are the lectures on Cassius Clay (the general, that is, not Mohammed Ali) and "The Most Orderly of Disorderly Houses" (still available on microfiche from the Lost Cause Press, Louisville). The latter deals with the colorful Lexington bawdy house operated for the first two decades of the 20th century by Belle Breezing in the most genteel tradition, the model for Belle Watling in *Gone with the Wind* (Mrs. Mitchell's husband was for a time on the staff of the Lexington *Leader*). The Aristophanic tradition is a common and invaluable property of western Europeans.

Menander, Alexis, and the other authors of the new comedy, and, in Rome, Plautus and Terence, presented the life of their times in a vein of exaggerated realism, but realism none the less. They tell us about the wicked pimp, the good-hearted whore-lady, or the virgins captured by pirates and sold into slavery for a fate worse than death. Of the latter group we cannot help being reminded of Robert Penn Warren's *Band of Angels,* the elaboration of the true story of a beautiful "high yellow" girl sold on the slave block on Cheapside in Lexington in the early 1850s. All were a part, but only a part, of ancient society. The scheming slave is a human type comparable to our Pompeiian guide, the sorry pimp a prototype of the evil characters who put Minnesota country girls on the streets of Manhattan. Menander, his contemporaries, and the Roman dramatists had their imitators in the 17th and 18th centuries, indeed, their superior is Molière, but they established a tradition that is a cornerstone of the modern comedy. The erotic is simply one aspect of human life, and its abuse is no less reprehensible than, say, the greed and irascibility of the *Dyskolos*.

A curious case of prurience in our time may be found in modern translations of Alciphron, an Athenian sophist of the second century A.D., whose letters were allegedly written by fourth century B.C. Athenians. In successful imitation of Lucian and with reminiscences of Menander and the new comedy, Alciphron composed the imaginary letters in a style that reflects vividly the life of his own age. Yet in modern times we have frequently elected to translate only that portion of the letters which are by the hetairai. None are particularly salacious and simply cover the gossip of kept ladies within their own circle.

To whom do these editions appeal? In the good old days of libraries when exact registries of borrowers were kept, we could identify the *Belesenheit* of all sorts of people from Thomas Carlyle to Studs Lonigan (who stole a book from a branch library as a gift to his girl friend). Circulation systems have changed, for the relief of librarians, to the detriment of literary historians who can no longer trace individual borrowing records. About a decade ago this writer found an old borrower's card in a translation of Alciphron's letters of the hetairai with the signatures of two English professors, a local geologist, a Pulitzer prize winning novelist, and himself (all from the 1930s). The card is now mounted carefully in a mint first edition of a novel by the penultimate borrower. One should not assume that the five recorded borrowers checked out the book from prurient interest (although I would not swear to it for myself). **It was simply the only translation of any part of Alciphron available in the library.**

There really isn't a great deal of difference between the nature of sexuality in ancient and modern literature and art. Ever since man came down from the trees he has been fascinated by the beauty of physical love, from passion in youth to mutual dedication in old age, but also by its ugliness and the sometimes grotesque humor in its animalistic aspects. The opulent upper class of the Roman Empire (possibly a small fraction of one percent of the population) included an element which indulged in all manner of hypersexuality, as Juvenal and Martial tell us, but no less than the *jeunesse dorée* of Britain's Hell-fire clubs of the 18th century and some of our contemporary motorcycle gangs. Many of the pantomimes of the Empire were vastly less respectable than Minsky's shows of the '30s and would have made Gypsy Rose Lee blush a deep crimson. Still, they were organized commercially on much the same basis. To quietly living Romans they were utterly gross, no less than the "topless and bottomless" joints of our times, when a much larger percentage of the population is considerably above the poverty level.

There were profligates of both sexes among the ancients. Of this group we probably know more about the Romans than the Greeks, thanks to the dedication of writers and artists of the Empire to gossip. The head of Marc Antony in the Uffizi in Florence shows a man with a haircut not much different from that of a contemporary lawyer. There is a mildly lustful gaze of his face, much better reflected in the gem attributed to one Arcellius depicting Marc Antony and the noted actress-courtesan Cytheris caressing each other in the buff in a one-horse sedan. Another surviving gem shows Marc Antony and Cleopatra on a Nile barge, again in birthday clothes. What kind of an inspiration might there have been for the often bawdy Shakespeare had he known these minuscule examples of ancient art!

The scandalous, often politically oriented literary references and graphic art of the Empire reflect a society with a leadership of questionable integrity. But the situation may not be much different from our own times when allegations, some factual, of alcoholic, sexual, or drug abuse by a public figure or a relative of a public figure are used to discredit that individual. There is a cameo ascribed to one Crateros showing Nero clad only in an animal skin, lustfully approaching five young boys and girls. In the Capitoline Museum in Rome there is a head of the youthful Nero, with a physiognomy apparently fully capable of the excesses ascribed to him by the historians and caricaturists. This sort of thing lasted to the end of the Empire, even showed up in Byzantium. Procopius told such vile stories about Theodora that my old teacher, Henry B. Dewing, was constrained to translate them into Latin rather than English for his Loeb edition.

It would be difficult to classify any literature that has survived from antiquity with the modern "adult" book or magazine. Even the mildly erotic late Greek novels, of which we have five, are more like soap opera. Apuleius and Petronius have raunchy scenes, but so do the best novelists throughout the ages. The erotic theater is a continuing phenomenon, although the erotic performances described by the Marquis de Sade and the junk on Times Square seem to go beyond anything known by the ancients, even some of Theodora's antics ascribed to her by Procopius. The erotic gems and cameos have their modern counterparts. There is a story that Augustus the Strong of Saxony became angry with one his mistresses, swore that every man in his realm would touch her body, and, to make sure, struck a coin showing her pudenda. Circulating today is a "heads and tails" quarter that shows up regularly in pool halls.

I prefer to think of the restraint and the sense of delicacy with which the best writers and artists of antiquity treated the beauty of love. Every time I read the *Aeneid* I am struck by Vergil's treatment of Dido's passion. A modern "adult" book author would have had a field day with the cave scene.

WORTH REPEATING

Articles of Interest
from the Non-Library Press

(Regularly a special column in *The Serials Librarian* which reprints articles of value from non-libary periodicals, this monographic supplement to *SL* provides a recent study of sex magazines published originally in *Medicine, Science and the Law*, Volume 18, No. 1, 1978. Reprinted with permission of the author and publisher.)

SEX MAGAZINES

J. J. Gayford

INTRODUCTION

The psychological effects of pornography have been reviewed by Crown (1973), Yaffe and Tennent (1973), and Kenyon (1975). Stoller (1970) postulates psychodynamic theories, while legal aspects are discussed by Grant (1973) and Hudson (1973). Gummer (1971) traces the development of the Obscene Publications Act of 1959, and the sale of sex literature throughout Europe and the United States. North (1974) makes a detailed study of fetish literature, but there is no up-to-date analysis of the contents of current sex magazines. In a psychosexual clinic, patients are frequently encountered who have consulted sex magazines in an attempt to solve their problems. It is proposed to review 72 magazines currently on sale.

Terminology

Pornography is an emotive term which is now associated with the Obscene Publications Act of 1959, and implies the moral judgment that the material is corrupt and depraved. Erotica infers that the material is of a milder nature and admits that it can be sexually stimulating; this would include 'girlie magazines,' which hints almost at an element of family approval. Sexually explicit material is a term in current usage which avoids moral judgment. Sex magazine is the term used by most patients, which implies that they find the content sexually stimulating, even though the majority of people may not.

ANALYSIS OF 72 MAGAZINES

Price

Seventy-two sex magazines were bought new and openly over the counter, for prices up to £1, at the end of 1976 and the beginning of 1977. The mean cost was 73p. S.D. ± 19.3p, with a range of 30p to the limit of £1. Size varied from 'pocket size,' 21 × 15 cm, to the larger magazine size 30 × 22 cm, and the number of pages varied from 30 to 200. So that some comparison could be made, the printed surface area of paper, excluding the cover, was calculated in square centimetres, and this was divided by the cost in pence. The resultant figure was called a 'value index.' This ranged from 187-1777, with a mean for the total sample of 655 S.D. ± 359 (see Figure 1). The use of colored illustrations is shown in Table 1 and also in Figure 1. This analysis excludes the cover, which in some cases bore the only color picture.

Subject Matter

Only one issue of each magazine was studied, but there appeared to be a distinctive style recurring throughout. In some cases the orientation of the publication was stated quite clearly on the cover. Broadly speaking, the magazines could be divided into those that depicted general erotica, and those that concentrated almost exclusively on some form of sexual deviancy. Within this group sado-masochism was common enough to be placed in a sub-group of its own.

The general erotica group were those that concentrated on describing heterosexual coitus, with the foreplay which went with this including cunnilingus and fellatio. This was the largest group and accounted for 44 (61%) of the sample. It also gave the best value for money in terms of printed material and photographs (Figure 1). Illustrations were generally of nude, or near-nude, females in various sexually provocative poses, and also included close up photographs of the female genitalia with the labia

TABLE 1

The Use of Color Illustrations in 72 Sex Magazines

	Erotica	Deviant	Sadomasochism
Color illustrations throughout the magazine	4 (5.6%)	0	0
Some color pages scattered throughout the magazine	3 (4.2%)	2 (2.8%)	4 (5.6%)
Center pages and cover contain the only color illustrations	5 (6. %)	12 (16.6%)	2 (2.9%)
No color illustrations, with the possible exception of the cover	32 (44.4%)	6 (8.3%)	2 (2.8%)
Total	44 (61.1%)	20 (27.7%)	8 (11.2%)

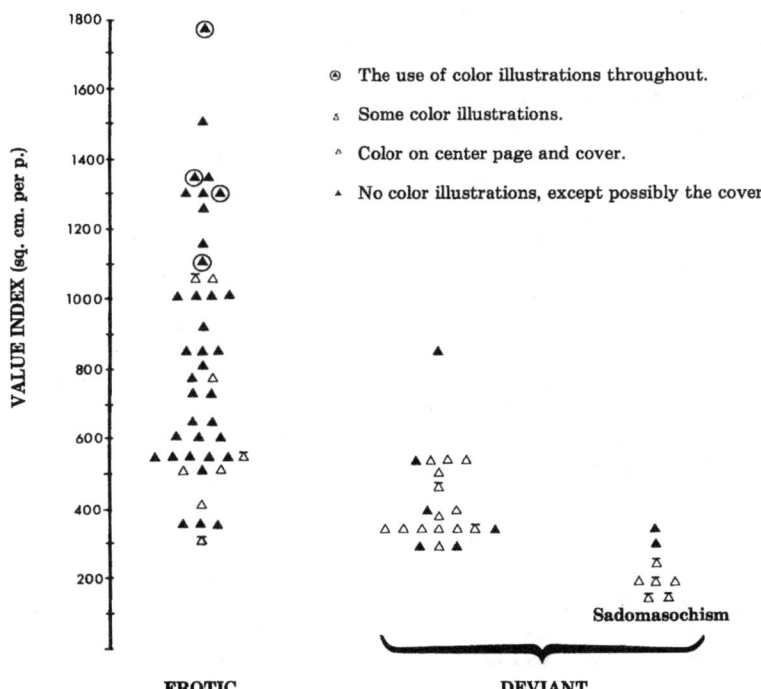

FIGURE 1. Diagram to Show the Value Index and Use of Colored Illustrations in 72 Sex Magazines.

held apart. Men, when they appeared, tended to play a secondary role, often with their genitalia covered by their nude female partner. Magazines featuring troilism, usually with two women, and those including lesbian features, were not excluded from this group, as it was not uncommon for such subject matter to appear occasionally.

The sexually deviant group was very mixed in its content and ranged from concentrating on a particular part of the female anatomy, such as breasts, legs, or buttocks, to transvestism and homosexuality. Three magazines concentrated on large breasts, and two on young girls. There was one exclusively male homosexual magazine. The main criterion for inclusion in this group was that coitus was rarely described and in many cases had become displaced by other activity. One fetish article simply described a woman trying on various pairs of gloves. In the magazine devoted solely to male homosexuality, this was described in terms of general relationships with no mention of sexual relations; this contrasted with the detailed account of the sex act in the so-called lesbian relationships described in several magazines. The magazines featuring young girls condemned paedophilia and made the point that all the girls photographed, although they looked young, were actually over 16. They were generally shown wearing an almost obsolete school uniform and in various stages of undress. Most of the stories and features related to sexual fantasy which was often bizarre. Twenty (28%) magazines were placed in the deviant group (Figure 1).

Eight (11%) magazines had an almost exclusive sado-masochistic content, with some fetish overlap. There were repeated descriptions of corporal punishment, some told in a historical setting. The female dominatrix featured prominently, but the subject matter was mainly confined to stories of young women receiving mild corporal punishment. Some authors went to great lengths to draw a distinction between their type of corporal punishment and sado-masochism, which they condemned. Photographs were supplemented with drawings in which clothing, posture, and the female figure were all greatly exaggerated. As can be seen from Figure 1, this group gave the lowest value index and less colored illustrations than the other groups.

Sale Restrictions

Fifty-four (75%) of the magazines stated on the cover that they were for adults only, or that they were not to be sold to persons under age. In some cases this was clearly printed in a distinctive color; one notable example was marked 'Not for sale or display to minors; keep out of the reach of children.' Of the 18 not marked for restricted sale one was notably the sole male homosexual journal.

Publishers and Editors

Forty-six (64%) were published at a London postal address, 16 (22%) in Surrey, and 8 (11%) were American publications produced under license in the United Kingdom. Only one did not state the publisher. Some publishers produced more than one magazine, and a number of publishers appeared to share the same address.

In 14 (19%) magazines no editor's name was stated, 32 (44%) had male editors, and 25 (35%) claimed female editors, although there were obvious pseudonyms. Editors were occasionally responsible for more than one publication.

Letters to the Editor and Readers' Contributions

Forty-one magazines (57%) carried correspondence columns. Some letters were extremely long and gave accounts of various sexual or para-sexual experiences. Letters were usually signed with a Christian name and the name of a town. Problems pages were run on similar lines, and the answers given varied from slick comments to a high degree of expertise. Some of the letters purported to have been sent by women. Photographs submitted by readers were a common feature and were usually of females in seductive or nude poses.

Advertising
Most magazines carried advertisements of some type, even if only to announce the next issue, to invite subscriptions, or to sell back numbers. Other magazines were advertised, especially those from the same company. Sex aids, books, and shops, together with sex films or tapes, were also commonly advertised, as were sauna and massage facilities, and even a domiciliary massage service. Only four magazines advertised non-sexual material such as cigarettes and radio equipment.

Contact Advertising
Fourteen (19%) magazines ran contact sections under box numbers. Usually a charge was made for this service, but some magazines offered this free to women. Most advertisements were for single people offering, or wanting, a particular type of sexual activity. Couples also advertised for group sexual activity, or for swapping sexual partners.

Professional Advisers
Nine (12.5%) magazines claimed to have professional advisers. One magazine published a list which filled the inside cover and included clergymen, urologists, sociologists, psychologists and psychiatrists. In most cases the adviser was a psychologist, but two magazines claimed to have a psychiatrist, and one an art adviser.

Cartoons, Sketches, and Reproductions of Graffiti
One third of the sample published sketches, cartoons, or reproductions of graffiti. Some tried to claim that pornography was an art, and produced 19th century classics to prove it. At the other end of the spectrum was pop art of sexual subjects, often luridly colored and using such photographic techniques as multiple exposure. Many of the drawings showed the sexual organs greatly enlarged. Cartoons on sexual topics varied a great deal and although some (for example, the more grotesque) were aimed at the publishers' exclusive readership, many were rather mild in character.

Titles of Magazines
Most magazines had short titles with sexual connotations. Exceptionally, there were titles which gave the impression that this was a scientific publication on sex. Others had two titles in an attempt to project both images. Obviously some magazines had undergone a radical change or had introduced color illustrations, and this was reflected in an appropriate prefix to the title.

Literary Style and Content

The content varied a great deal, ranging from magazines written in good English and with a wide use of vocabulary, to those with poorly constructed sentences interspersed between pictures. Certain sexual or parasexual words appeared again and again with boring repetition. Typographical errors were more common than in most journals. Few magazines could resist the temptation to claim they were the best in their field. A strong anti-establishment theme came across in some journals. Even English publications tried on occasion to produce an American style. Pictorial material played a variable part and was of very variable quality. Frequently the pictures and the text bore little relation to each other. Some magazines carried nonsexual articles and there were cases where the author seemed prepared to discuss any topic in order to fill his allotted space.

Recurrent themes were the sexual exploits of bored housewives, confessions of prostitutes, and tales of how virginity has been lost. The reporting of a supposed sexual underworld in what is reputed to be a respectable section of society is a particular delight of some publishers. Much of what is written has an element of fantasy about it, often in a luxurious, sophisticated or historical setting. In contrast, others have a crude, earthy setting, with equally crude descriptions of sexual acts. Little attention is paid to morals, conscience, or relationships, other than sexual relationships. Contraception is rarely mentioned and pregnancy never seems to occur. In fairness, however, some articles do stress that contraception has been used.

DISCUSSION

By limiting the price paid, and only sampling new literature bought openly, the sample was skewed in favor of so-called 'soft pornography.' More expensive American and Scandinavian literature was in evidence in sealed packages, giving the impression that this was 'stronger' material. Figure 2 shows that it can be difficult to define the boundaries between erotica and other magazines, with modern women's magazines carrying more and more articles on sexual topics.

Sex magazines of the type sampled appear to be readily available and often prominently displayed, although there is some attempt made to limit sales to adults only. It is difficult to assess the effect of this type of literature on young people. Certainly there is a great demand for clear instruction on sexual and erotic techniques. The real issue seems to be the moral and judgmental one of whether sex magazines will corrupt and deprave young people. Youngsters acquiring their sexual techniques from the magazines reviewed would appear to learn to make rapid, bold sexual advances, with speedy progression to oro-genital contact; they would be exposed to sexual practices which most people would consider deviant, and would learn almost nothing about relationships and sexual

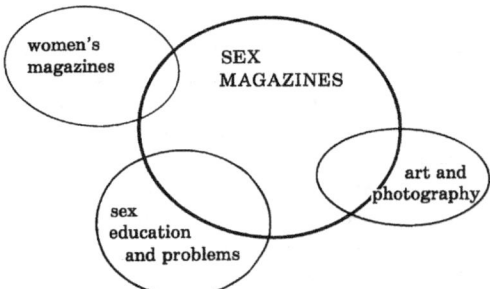

FIGURE 2. Diagram to Show the Overlap Between Sex Magazines and Other Magazines.

responsibility. However, having said this, there can only be doubts about how a more idealistic journal would fare in the competitive commercial world of sex magazines.

The measurement of value index and the number of colored illustrations is only a crude quantitative index; no attempt was made to evaluate qualitative or sexually stimulating characteristics. It would appear on these criteria that those magazines with the widest circulation were able to give more printed and colored pictures. The more deviant magazines, with presumably a smaller, more selective readership, gave less printed material and there was less chance of finding colored illustrations.

Griffitt et al. (1974) and Mann et al. (1974) show that, at least over a short period of time, both male and female readers of erotic literature experience increased sexual activity. Yaffe and Tennent (1973), in reviewing the effects of sexually explicit material, not only reported that 84% of males and 69% of females over the age of 21 have been exposed to this medium, but the majority found it initially sexually exciting. Obviously what stimulates one person may not excite another. Byrne et al. (1973) found that there was a correlation between husband and wife response to sexually explicit material, both in its erotic effects and in their moral judgment. Authoritarians found it more sexually exciting but were also more ready to condemn on moral grounds. Izard and Caplan (1974) agreed that the majority of sex magazines are bought by men during the highly active phase of their sex lives (25-45 years.) Women, although they will not usually buy sex magazines, are not averse to reading them, and can find them sexually stimulating.

There are now a number of ways in which sexually exciting material can be used in sex therapy (Gillan & Gillan, 1976), even if it is only to start a couple talking about sex. This stimulates sexual response, which in turn can be translated into sexual relations. The introduction of new sexual ideas may not persuade the couple to try that practice, but the mere discussion of the topic, even if rejected, can lead to improved enjoyment of sexual relations.

North (1974), in his review of the fetish literature, comments on its overlap with sado-masochism. He also comments on the amateur standard of production, with duplicated pages interspersed with black and white photographs. This is contrasted with glossy magazines from America on the same subject. Clearly the standard of British literature on the subject has increased and improved in quality, at least in terms of production. There is still an import of American productions of this type, but usually at a price of over £2. The advertisements in these American magazines show that there are many journals on these subjects. Surprisingly, there are even clandestine private magazines, the printers and publishers of which are not acknowledged, which mimic these American glossy magazines and are marketed at a similar price. A technique used by most magazines, including the majority of those reviewed, is to avoid displaying the date of publication in a prominent place. This means that a magazine bought as new, in a sealed, transparent package, may have been published two or three years before.

With over half the magazines carrying correspondence columns, considerable reader participation could be claimed. Where sexual problems were discussed seriously, the problems presented were similar in character to those seen in the psychosexual clinic. The best of answers, often from professionals, presented fair counsel. There certainly seems to be a need for this type of service, where advice can be sought on an anonymous basis. Obviously this does not allow for full exploration, and even well meaning advice can be misguided under these circumstances. Even so, to dismiss the whole correspondence section as the work of the editorial staff would be to attribute them with extremely fertile imaginations.

Contact advertisements evoked mixed feelings. At best they could be seen as appeals from lonely people seeking sexual partners sympathetic to their needs. However, althought the publishers claim they try to prevent prostitutes from using these facilities, they have to admit that it does happen, and although money is not mentioned, the way in which some women offer their services must give rise to some suspicion. The impression gained was that these were appeals for sexual relationships, often of a deviant nature, from people hoping to find a willing partner with similar tendencies, thus avoiding all the complications which might result from seeking such a relationship in a normal social setting.

Drawings, as opposed to photographs, appeared in one third of the magazines, ranging from the type of graffiti commonly found on lavatory walls, to the obsessional qualities of the tatooist. The more deviant literature had to rely more heavily on drawings, which can portray a bizarre fantasy beyond the bounds of reality, and the scope of photography. Women with exaggeratedly slim waists, pronounced breasts and long legs could therefore be depicted striking anatomically impossible poses in garments it would be difficult to wear.

In his analysis of pornography, Kenyon (1975) discusses the subject under six headings:

1. *Cathartic:* providing a safety valve for outlet of sexual fantasy without translating this into reality;
2. *Aversive:* deflecting the reader from a particular sexual practice which would vary according to the subject and the person viewing it;
3. *Stimulant:* putting ideas into readers' minds and even encouraging them to try for themselves;
4. *Corrupting:* encouraging a person to act against his moral principles;
5. *Liberating:* claiming that it may be good for us to be shocked, or at least to rethink our ideals, prejudices, taboos, and customs; and
6. *No important effect:* in that pornography quickly bores, and is only of appeal because it is the forbidden fruit.

Some of these ideas are diametrically opposed and cannot both be true for the same person viewing a particular topic at a particular time. Yet there has only to be a small change of subject, or a lapse of time, for what may at first have produced aversion to become stimulating. Some might see this as having a subtly corrupting effect, whereas others may see it as liberalization.

When a person found guilty of a heinous crime is also found to possess a library of pornographic literature an association is often made between the two. There is no way of telling how many people have such a library and yet do not commit crimes. It would be just as logical, but equally unproven, to claim that a library of pornographic magazines has prevented them from committing sex offences. Even so, Crown (1973) has a point when he claims that sex which uses literature as a stimulus replaces relationships with people. Kenyon (1975) counters this argument by pointing out that sex literature can be of help to those who are sexually disabled for physical, psychological, or social reasons, and who can find no partner to satisfy them sexually. There can be little doubt that sex literature provides masturbatory fantasy for males, but this can be used therapeutically for a masturbatory training program which leads in gradual stages from an unacceptable deviant pattern of behavior towards more rewarding and acceptable sexual practice.

Both Eysenck (1976) and Stoller (1976), although representing very differnt viewpoints, would agree that the effects of pornography are underresearched. Eysenck goes on to suggest that, like drug manufacturers, the publishers of pornography should show how a responsible attitude and finance such research from their profits.

The recruitment of professional advisers and the use of titles, or subtitles, suggesting that the publication is a scientific journal, shows that the magazines are seeking respectability. Anyone working in the psychosexual field would find it difficult to dismiss the whole cult of sex magazines as irrelevant to the subject. It is impossible to know if people are helped from this source to solve their problems. Kenyon (1975) suggests that better education, rather than censorship and legislation, would make pornography seem in poor taste, rather than something to be feared. It would appear that sexually explicit material has a valid place in our society, provided there is control of standard and use.

REFERENCES

Byrne D., Cherry F., Lamberth J. and Mitchell H. E. (1973) Husband-wife similarity in response to erotic stimuli. *J. Personality 41,* 385-394.
Crown S. (1973) Pornography and sexual promiscuity. *Med. Sci. Law 13,* 239-243.
Eysenck H. J. (1976) *Sex and Personality.* Open Books, London.
Gillan P. and Gillan R. (1976) *Sex Therapy Today.* Open Books, London.
Grant J. H. (1973) Pornography. *Med. Sci. Law 13,* 232-238.
Griffitt W., May J. and Veitch R. (1974) Sexual stimulation and interpersonal behaviour. *J. Personality Soc. Psychol 30,* 367-377.
Gummer J. S. (1971) *The Permissive Society: Fact or Fantasy.* Cassel, London.
Hudson W. M. F. (1973) Pornography and the law. *Med. Sci. Law 13,* 244-245.
Izard C. E. and Caplan S. (1974) Sex difference in emotional response to erotic literature. *J. Consulting Clin. Psychol. 42,* 468.
Kenyon F. E. (1975) Pornography, the law and mental health. *Brit. J. Psychiatry 126,* 225-233.
Mann J., Berkowitz L., Sidman J., Starr S. and West S. (1974) Satiation of transient stimulating effects of erotic films. *J. Personality Soc. Psychol. 30,* 729-735.
North M. (1974) *The Outer Fringe of Sex.* London, The Odyssey Press.
Stoller R. J. (1976) *Perversion, the Erotic Form of Hatred.* The Harvester Press Ltd.
Yaffe M. and Tennent G. (1973) Pornography: A psychological appraisal. *Brit. J. Hosp. Med. 9,* 379-386.

SEX MAGAZINES: PROBLEMS OF ACQUISITION, RETENTION, DISPLAY, AND DEFENSE IN PUBLIC AND ACADEMIC LIBRARIES

Bruce A. Shuman
Karen Dalziel Tallman

When the authors of this article were first asked by the editor of *The Serials Librarian* to undertake this assignment, they thought that they knew something of the scope and nature of sex magazines. Wrong. Perusal of the shelves of several bookstores and magazine racks in several cities persuaded the authors that there was much that they could not have imagined being sold over counters, and that there is literally a periodical for *every* erotic taste, ranging from the tame and slightly risqué to the almost unbelievable, in terms of content, emphasis, or graphic depiction of the topic. It became, therefore, incumbent upon the authors to pare down the very broad classification sex magazines, to something manageable, and to something which would be of concern to libraries. This was accomplished in several ways, as will become apparent from all that follows.

A look at class 1360 of *The Standard Periodical Directory* (6th edition, 1979/80) reveals that there are just about 100 periodical titles fitting the category, "Men's Adventure and Detective." "Sex Magazines" is not a topic chosen by the *Directory,* but class 1360, together with other subsets, such as "Women's Magazines" and "Homosexual Literature," pretty well cover the field of titles concerned wholly or partly with that subject we call sex. The authors quickly realized that some judicious cutting of the topic was necessary, and somewhat arbitrarily elected, in this article, at least, to discuss only those periodicals which covered male, heterosexual sexuality, as represented by space "a" in Figure 1.

However, a further diagram is necessary, showing the critical path the authors took to the subset of magazines scrutinized in this article. This path is represented by the wide line in Figure 2.

The subject of this article, then, is that class of male, heterosexual-oriented magazines dealing with sex and sexuality, at least in part, which are indexed (and therefore of most value to libraries) in one or more commonly-found popular periodicals indexes. One title, *Players,* is indexed, but caters to the "urban, black male," and was excluded from this study as not sufficiently general. One other title, while unindexed, is often discussed and widely read, but *Hustler* was excluded from this study, due to its difficulty of access, as unindexed, rather than for its at-

FIGURE 1. A Classification of "Sex Magazines."

Audience:	Men	Women	Both Sexes
Affiliation: "Straight"	a	b	c*
"Gay"	d	e	

*Examples: art, photography, sexuality in general

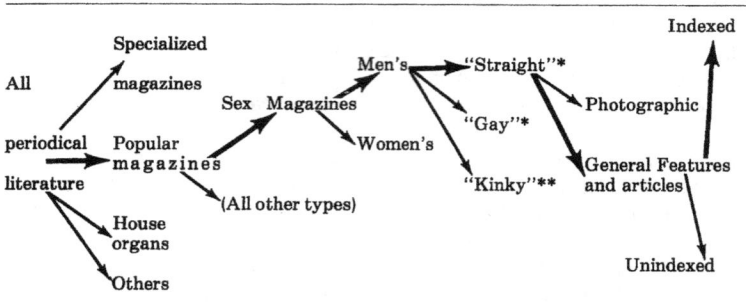

FIGURE 2: Classification of Periodicals, Showing Critical Path Taken to Provide Topic of Article

* The terms "straight" and "gay" are so widely used in common parlance that they are self-explanatory.

** The term "kinky" refers to those titles which emphasize the bizarre or the unusual in eroticism. Further definition is difficult, but some empirical research will show that there is a kinky magazine for every kink.

titudes, contents, or displays. A few indexed magazines (e.g., *Guns and Ammo, True, Saga)* will occasionally carry a photographic layout or discussion of sexuality, but were excluded as being primarily devoted to the outdoor life, hunting, fishing, and other male-bonding activity, rather than heterosexual intimate behavior, which is the focus of the magazines which do enter the category we are left with: *Playboy, Penthouse,* and *Oui.*

Once those three titles were identified, a test of controversiality was sought, such that the authors could verify that libraries in general, and academic and public libraries specifically, would find them classed as controversial by at least some patrons.

Such a test was derived from the pages of the American Library Association's *Newsletter on Intellectual Freedom,* which chronicles and updates controversies in libraries, the media, the arts, and in general. Table 1 represents problems encountered by libraries due to the presence of *Playboy, Penthouse,* and/or *Oui* on library shelves over the past three years.

Convinced now that the three periodical titles are potentially or actually troublesome for libraries, the authors are ready to proceed to the thorny area of definitional matters. Prior to the actual discussion of our topic, we wish to describe and portray the phyla, genera, and species with which we shall be working. These *heterosexual men's magazines* consist of a broad variety of articles, dealing with politics, lifestyles, sexual mores, adventures, and leisure, always accompanied by interviews, humor, cartoons, and fiction of high quality. Also *de rigeur* in the three titles under investigation are photographic layouts which show extremely attractive females in full frontal nudity (as well as back and side views, etc.). Other

TABLE 1
Periodical Titles Challenged (indexed only) in Libraries in the U.S.,
as Reported by the *Newsletter on Intellectual Freedom,*
April, 1976 to April, 1979, with Indexing of Titles

PLAYBOY*	PENTHOUSE**	OUI**
(ten incidents)	(eleven incidents)	(eight incidents)
Atlanta, GA	Atlanta, GA	Atlanta, GA
Greencastle, PA	Benton, KY	Benton, KY
Cleveland, OH	Cleveland, OH	Cleveland, OH
Columbia, SC	Manchester, NH	Columbia, SC
Flint, MI	Columbia, SC	Flint, MI
Franklin, KY	Flint, MI	Oklahoma City, OK
Oklahoma City, OK	Franklin, KY	St. Louis, MO
St Louis, MO	Oklahoma City, OK	Alexandria, LA
Belleville, IL	St. Louis, MO	
Mt. Vernon, IA	Los Angeles, CA	
	Belleville, IL	

* *Playboy* is indexed in *Access, Magazine Index, Monthly Periodicals Index* and *Popular Periodicals Index.*
** *Penthouse* and *Oui* are indexed in *Access* and *Magazine Index.*

heterosexual men's magazines, however, may de-emphasize words, pile on the photographs, and emphasize specific parts of the female body. One magazine portrays itself, for example, as "the magazine of the D-cups." Others seem to highlight genitalia, derrierès, bondage and restraint, obesity, pre-pubescence or even blood. Real or simulated? Don't ask.

In fact, given access to the complete run of English-language, American men's magazines, one might safely say that there are perhaps a dozen classifications which can be made on the bases of audience targeted, emphasis of editorial or photographic material, price, or quality. The only family resemblance would seem to lie in the appreciation for the undraped female body which pervades all of them. Beyond that, the variation is enormous, and the effects are, like beauty, in the eye of the beholder. Nonetheless, a few generalized assumptions are in order:

1. The law (state, municipal, or federal) does not attempt to define sex magazines, *per se,* preferring to proscribe or list the things such magazines cannot depict or represent and still be considered "legal." Sex magazines, therefore, would appear to be defined only by those who read them, enjoy them, publish them, avoid them, crusade for or against them, or acquire them for collections. After all, the proportion of sexually-oriented content may vary from title to title, and even from issue to issue, and there is no consensus about what constitutes sexual display. *Newsweek,* for example, may run a photograph of a topless waitress. *Sports Illustrated* annually features a spread on the latest in women's swimwear which leaves little to the imagination. As intent of the publisher is hard to devine and extremely difficult to prove, we are left with the inescapable conclusion that a magazine is a "sex magazine" if you think it is.

2. People may react differently to identical stimuli, and a photograph or joke which offends one reader to the point of fury or total embarrassment, may leave a second reader rolling with laughter and a third puzzled or completely unaffected. Put another way, each of us has his or her "gross-out point," and there's no accounting for taste.

3. As this article concerns libraries (or will shortly) and the authors are librarians, our next logical question is that of whether libraries tend to subscribe to *Playboy, Penthouse,* and *Oui,* or think it prudent or financially necessary to leave them alone. Our conclusion is that decisions concerning whether or not to subscribe to such titles are normally made on a cost/benefit matrix, rather than as a result of doctrinaire disapproval or popular sentiment. Indexing of all three titles is, of course, a point in their favor. The expense of their subscriptions, their accessioning, and binding could not normally be justified unless they are of use in retrieval of specific information (as indexing permits), as well as for leisure and recreational uses. Donations of such popular periodicals, while they may obviate the cost of subscriptions, still require an ongoing commitment to the magazines, in terms of retention, preservation, and binding.

4. At least one scholar warns that it is erroneous and shortsighted of librarians to assume that *Playboy, Penthouse,* and *Oui* are three manifestations of the same interest. Lee D. Rossi[1] observes that, upon careful examination, a difference in photographic subjects can be observed between *Playboy* and the other two titles. Rossi contends that the nude women in *Playboy* are "treated with some of the same reverence that Americans ordinarily reserve for the flag, motherhood, and God." *Playboy* women, says Rossi, have flawless bodies, with any blemishes or signs of imperfection tastefully airbrushed away. "They represent the ideal woman of American culture . . . They are all cheerful and healthy, and one suspects them of latent chastity. They are airbrushed madonnas." The women shown in *Penthouse* and *Oui,* on the other hand, "embody a decadent sexuality which is a lot more exciting . . . They are much more voluptuous, world-weary and tough than the girl-next-door . . . they don't need an airbrush; they're sexy just the way they are . . . you can see the wrinkles and birthmarks . . . they're older than the models in *Playboy* and their breasts sag a bit." While Rossi's observations are interesting, verification of his contention is left to the reader. At least there is partial evidence to support a claim that *Playboy, Penthouse,* and *Oui* are not clones of one another, and that separate trials may be more in keeping with jurisprudential fairness.

5. One nagging question which will not go away without discussion, is "What is obscene?" This question has been asked through history (but never answered to everyone's satisfaction) by judges, juries, law enforcement agencies, booksellers, libraries, and, probably by you. Libraries need to know so that they can keep on the safe and permissible side of the law; and you need to think about it, so that you can formulate some sort of appropriate response to those who assail your library for having standards too low, too high, or no standards at all. Even now, the U.S. 5th Circuit Court of Appeals is studying a case[2] which is designed to test whether a magazine (like any of our sample) may be declared obscene (and thus illegal) because one or more of its articles or features is found by a judge and/or a jury to exceed contemporary community standards relating to sex. Unfortunately, there are members of the library community who feel no need of pondering or asking this question: they already know. Fiske[3] and Busha[4] conducted studies to show that, in many cases, the staunchest foes of freedom to acquire and display such titles as *Playboy, Penthouse,* and *Oui* are librarians themselves. Librarians are people too, and, as such, they may feel that they are perfectly capable of sorting out smut from worthwhile reading matter. Eli Oboler's excellent *The Fear of the Word*[5] contains a readable and mordant discussion of these problems libraries face, and is recommended reading.

Anyway, no library can afford to dismiss the question of obscenity without careful deliberation, principally because the community will not let the librarians do so. Slogans like "contemporary community standards," "traditional values," "clear and present danger," and even "save our children" will be employed by free-lance moralists to provide them with enough popular support to gain leverage over a library's selection procedures and policies.

Few writers have been so rash as to attempt a working definition of obscenity or pornography, and the authors have only found one they agree with completely. That definition (actually a non-definition) comes from Mr. Justice Potter Stewart of the United States Supreme Court, who, after regretfully admitting that he could never succeed in defining it (the censorable), allowed as how "I know it when I see it." In search of something which could be used as a checklist, for grading of the three titles at hand, however, the authors turned to Robert Liston,[6] who gives a nine-point definition of pornography in his *The Right to Know: Censorship in America*. Table 2 provides Liston's definitional points, with an evaluative comment after each, as viewed by the authors, for *Playboy*, *Penthouse*, and *Oui*, taken, despite Rossi's possible objection, as a single class of titles.

Thus, a scorecard for the three titles in the class often purchased by libraries would appear to reveal that, to many people, the titles are seen as pornographic. In six of the nine criteria, the magazines score positive-

TABLE 2
Measurement of *Playboy, Penthouse,* and *Oui* on Liston's Stated Definitional Criteria

Liston's criteria for determining whether a book or periodical is pornographic:	Scorecard for *Playboy, Penthouse* and *Oui*
1. The subject matter relates to sex	Predominantly, yes.
2. It is a public display of sexual activity	Again, yes, but depends on one's definition of "activity."
3. A monetary fee is involved	Models depicted are handsomely rewarded.
4. There is an absence of love	Arguable, but generally true, as the viewer may lust or admire, but never love.
5. It is a phenomenon of males	Women read these magazines, but the vast majority of readership is male.
6. It exploits women	Arguments for and against are possible.
7. It engenders guilt	Too individualistic to evaluate.
8. The sensitivities of some people are affronted	Definitely so.
9. It involves the arts and demeans them	Involvement *si!* As to whether they are demeaned, only the reader can judge.

ly; with the other three statements, of necessity, judgment calls. A review of recent issues of the *Newsletter on Intellectual Freedom* is persuasive that many communities are riven because their libraries contain such material, and for many of the reasons offered by Liston.

But we still haven't settled the question of pornography. As Jay Daily says in his *Anatomy of Censorship*,[7] "Special kinds of erotica that can be called pornography must follow a pattern of going from a simple and permissible act to one that represents the ultimate in sinfulness. This naturally varies with the readership at which the author directs his work." Later in the same book,[8] Daily states that "A necessary part of pornography is the happy violation of taboos, and a work that includes repentance and regret can no longer deliver the shock the reader is waiting for." Nor is obscenity in the groin of the beholder, asserts Daily. "It is in the brain of everyone as a part of our ability to communicate. What is obscene is the class of messages we reject without any attempt to understand or give an indication that we have received the message."[9] Clearly, *Playboy* and its analogues qualify as pornography when viewed by persons such as those whom Daily depicts—those who have closed off any attempt to understand, and who prefer to despise and condemn. For the rest of us, such magazines may be erotic, in the positive sense of arousing pleasurable feelings, but are not classed as pornographic, in the negative sense of filthy, dangerous, or fit for burning.

PUBLIC LIBRARIES AND SEX MAGAZINES

If put to it, one may enumerate fairly impressive lists of reasons both for and against the purchase of such magazines for public libraries, which must serve the entire populace, from pre-schoolers to senior citizens. The authors enumerate below some of the more persuasive arguments for purchasing them:

1. *Demand.* Playboy and the other magazines are enormously popular in most communities, and patrons of the library ought to be able to expect them to be made available at public expense.

2. *Indexing.* The three titles concerned are all indexed through two or more commonly-found indexing services. *Playboy's* contents are actually accessible through four services.

3. *Intellectual Freedom.* To refuse to purchase such popular magazines out of fear of reprisal is, in a real sense, caving in to the demands of censors and others who feel that they should and must set the moral tone for the community.

4. *Changing Mores.* Words, images, and photographic depictions seen as taboo in all segments of society only a decade or two ago are now reasonably commonplace, as witness the acceptance of such words as "crap," "boobs," and "buns" on popular television shows, together with growing lists of adherents to alternative life styles and other modern

phenomena which have lost their shock value. Those who gasped when Rhett told Scarlett that frankly, he didn't give a damn! now may shudder internally but do not seethe with outrage when an American president boasts that, should a touted rival decide to oppose him, he'd "whip his ass."

5. *Flexibility.* A library with a sense of compromise may often manage to retain and make available subscriptions to such magazines. It is possible to strike a deal with those who protest by agreeing to place such subscriptions on high shelves, behind the counter, away from the children's collection, or in a locked case. Such agreements may violate the *letter* of intellectual freedom, but the spirit is preserved in that the library still has the consent of the community to buy, keep, and make accessible those titles.

6. *Definitional Problems.* Librarians who feel brave may challenge any individual or group likely to protest inclusion of such titles to show that they are obscene or pornographic. Few, as has already been stated, can come up with anything coherent and meaningful which defines that class of periodicals, and distinguishes it from the permissible and innocuous. This game is risky, however, as the patron may decide that numbers are the test of significance, and may return with 100 or so concerned parents or loyal Americans who all solemnly agree that these magazines are dirty. Watch yourself!

On the other side of the ledger, an impressive list of reasons *not* to acquire *Playboy* (or anything like it) may be marshalled:

1. *Cost.* The prices of subscriptions to all magazines have soared in recent years. The library's budget, except in a few isolated cases, has not kept pace. Postage, too, has escalated the cost of acquiring such titles, which normally need special handling and protection, once in the library's collection. They may have to be locked away and signed out for, like other high-ripoff titles such as *Chilton's* and *Audel's* auto repair books.

2. *Problems with Organized Groups.* Religious groups find such magazines to be prime targets for hatred. Politicians in search of issues often fasten on pornography as a target of opportunity. (There is nothing harder to defend than "smut," once it is so labeled in the popular mind.) Feminist groups may see *Playboy* and its "philosophy" as detrimental to the cause of sexual equality. *Playboy* glorifies female bodies, but often treats the women inside, they say, as accessories for the stylish male.

3. *Qualitative Judgments.* It is legitimate to argue that a library's money is better spent on other materials, provided that one sets out clearly what is better, and why.

4. *Law Enforcement Agencies.* These may feel strongly that perusal of such titles by the young or the susceptible may have a direct bearing on the incidence of rape and other sex and violent crimes in the community. Such agencies, especially in conjunction with other organized groups,

may bring on libraries the difficult choice of "defending smut" or caving in to those who feel that the first place to begin sanitizing the community is down at the library, where they put all those girlie magazines out on the racks where anyone can see them.

5. *Parents.* Parents concerned for their children (or *everybody's* children) often wish to protect the young from the stark realities of sex until they are old enough to understand that responsibility often accompanies desire. Triple-page fold-outs showing abundantly-proportioned women in complete or prevailing undress are difficult to defend against irate mothers and fathers who are deeply concerned about their families, and what the world's coming to in general.

6. *Privacy.* It often becomes necessary to secure such magazines against theft or mutilation. This often occasions the need for sign-out sheets, requiring that the borrower write his (or her) name and address when looking at sex magazines, a condition which could lead to embarrassment when others happen to see their names.

7. *Librarians.* Yes, librarians, and for many reasons. Personal values often influence selection, and librarians, being a generally conservative lot, may feel that the purchase of *Playboy* or the others constitutes an act which may be wrong, unwarranted, dangerous to the common welfare, or simply unnecessary, as the bus station and two local bookstores are happy to sell them to anyone with the price. Also, librarians have much to lose in running afoul of politicians in #2, who may view their insistence on the right to read freely as an obstacle to a "Clean Up Our City Now" campaign.

As the reader can see, the lists are *both* persuasive, appealing to the natural urge of the librarian to keep his or her job and to the librarian's sense of integrity and mission. Any or all arguments may be marshalled as support for whatever decision one makes, and the specific realities of one's situation may turn out to be the ultimate determinant of what is "right" or "wrong."

In preparing the "backgrounder" prior to undertaking this article, the authors scurried out, in their respective communities, to view and evaluate the titles likely for inclusion in such an investigation. A careful scrutiny of the three titles under discussion allows another "report card" for subject matter, on certain categories commonly thought to be ingredients of obscenity, as is seen in Table 3.

While flipping through the range of sex magazines available will reveal all of the depictions and more, the three titles available through indexing contain only about one-half of the stimuli. Even then, several of the criteria must be defined, like obscenity, by the individual. Degradation of women, for example, is a particularly sensitive point in many communities, and one group of those consulted may find *Playboy* centerfolds appalling, while a second groups finds them flattering to women in general, and a third group mildly wonders what all the shouting is about.

Speaking broadly, censorship tends to be a phenomenon of the poorly-

TABLE 3
Representations Commonly Found in Men's Sex Magazines, with Scorecard for *Playboy, Penthouse,* and *Oui*

Criterion of Pornography	Found in *Playboy, Penthouse,* and *Oui*
1. Display of female breasts	always
2. Display of female pubic hair	always
3. Display of female genitalia	sometimes
4. Woman in blatantly sexually inviting pose	always
5. Suggested female masturbation	sometimes
6. Woman with man in sexual pose	very rarely
7. Two or more nude women together	sometimes
8. Overweight, grotesque or deformed women	never
9. Fetishistic photographs (garter belts excluded)	rarely
10. Nude or semi-nude person in restraints	rarely
11. Whips or other implements of pain or violence	never
12. Degradation of women	(open to interpretation)
13. Anal emphasis/excrement	never
14. Bestiality	never
15. Homosexual representation	never (except for humorous effect)
16. Blood in any context	never

educated and easily swayed. Yet censorship seems a part of every established religious group in America. One argument in favor of censorship of such magazines as we are discussing, however, comes to us from an eminent and respected sociologist, Ernest van den Haag: "If we indulge pornography, and do not allow censorship to restrict it, our society at best will become even more coarse, brutal, anxious, indifferent, deindividualized, hedonistic; at worst, its ethos will disintegrate altogether."[10]

While such argument is easy to see as sheer hyperbole or too simplistic, it has apparently persuaded many of every community's residents (who probably arrived at the same conclusions without benefit of sociological perspective) to act. Van den Haag and Everyman, your neighbor down the block, join forces on this issue: they are not acting as repressive censors, they are acting in an attempt to save you, save the children, and save the *society* in which we live, whether we wish it or not. It is their sacred duty to protect us against that which can and will harm us, and if we are too shortsighted to see that they act in our best interests, they're just going to have to go and do it anyway. It is our whole culture they're fighting for, and the outcome of their struggle (German = *Kampf*) will affect all of us and everything.

Tactics of the censor may vary, but for the censor to prevail in a community, and be given *carte blanche* to eradicate that which is filthy and degraded from the city library's shelves, several conditions must obtain:

1. *Conduciveness.* Changing community values, escalating crime rates, venereal disease rates, teenage pregnancy rates, together with the ob-

vious presence of new sex roles and new freedom, cause dislocation and anxiety in the community.

2. *Provocation.* This varies, but usually, a crusade for cleanliness in the library's collection proceeds out of some horrible incident. Should the apartment of the latest mass-murder/sex-slayer turn out to have in it neatly stacked issues of *Playboy* or *Penthouse,* or should police discover a wall full of defaced centerfolds, the *vigilantes* have what they need to get into motion: clear and present danger.

3. *Mobilization of Participants.* A newspaper editor, a local minister, parents of a murdered girl, a politician, or any other charismatic or sympathetic character can easily turn the presence of sex magazines on library shelves into an "issue." Some influential contributors, the selection of an impressive name (e.g., Coalition to Save Our Kids), and accusations of "filth" and "smut" levelled against the library, and it may well become *sauve qui peut* for the librarians.

4. *Rationalizations.* At times, a mass rally against "immorality" may be less effective as a tactic than a subtle approach to the librarian, in the name of God, community safety, patriotism, or whatever comes to mind. "Just give us this one magazine," they intone righteously, "and we'll go away contented." But remember: to appease such groups by surrendering one title today sets a dangerous precedent, and almost inevitably means more trouble tomorrow. Tomorrow, when they come to your library with a rented truck and a "laundry list" of "dangerous and indecent" book and periodical titles which some or all of them worry about, it's too late to climb up on your Library Bill of Rights. *Vox populi, vox dei,* you know. You have little choice but to accede to their wishes and try to salvage what you can. Of course, as has been pointed out, librarians are often in perfect agreement with those who rail against *Playboy*, etc., and are secretly or openly relieved that someone else has removed the onerous burden of "censor" from their shoulders. One more point, in the context of rationalization: "censor" is not a word which anyone uses in referring to oneself. A watchdog, a guardian, an older-and-wiser head, but never a censor. A censor is always someone else, someone one doesn't like or agree with.

EFFECTIVE COUNTERMEASURES FOR LIBRARIES (EMPIRICAL ONLY; NO GUARANTEES)

First and foremost, remain calm. Don't get excited, terrified, or overly defensive. Find out existing local laws, and determine whether you are on the permissible side of them. Consult with an attorney to determine your culpability, should a suit be brought. Counterattack by pointing out to all who will listen that the magazines in question have published interviews with such notables as Jimmy Carter,

Anita Bryant, and Teilhard de Chardin. Emphasize that those who are offended or upset at viewing total female nudity are not obliged to look, and that no conclusive evidence has ever been brought forth which links reading of sex magazines with commission of sex crime. Until causality can be found, demand that those who have charges to bring against such magazines permit the usual presumption of innocence, as our civil law requires.

Cultivate friends. Remember that, depending upon shading of words chosen and interpretations, a newspaper editorial or article can make you, the city librarian, look like either a shining beacon of intellectual freedom in a time of encroaching repression, or a pandering smut-peddler, attempting to contribute to the delinquency of minors through the placement and availability of loathesome magazines on open shelves. Get to know forward-looking local attorneys, and hobnob, if possible, with those in newspapers and other media of communication. The Office for Intellectual Freedom of the ALA is there to advise in such cases, so give them a call, and consult with the American (or local) Civil Liberties Union, if your hassle becomes a court case. Good public relations can go a long way toward defusing such a situation while it is still potential. It is demonstrably easier to attack in print and from the pulpit an anonymous libertine down at the library than it is to accuse a friend and dedicated public servant of corrupting the morals of the community. Finally, have a Friends of the Library group in place, *before* the emergency arises.

Don't weaken. Stick up for what you believe in. You'll be amazed and gratified at the numbers of citizens who will come to your defense if they see you as protecting their (and everyone's) right to read freely, against the forces of darkness and the book-burners. Naturally, all of this is easy enough for us to say. Decisions affecting *your* job and *your* standing in the community will have to proceed from your convictions and your unique set of circumstances, opportunities, and constraints.

ACADEMIC LIBRARIES AND SEX MAGAZINES

Problems of Acquisitions and Selection

In academic situations, selection of materials is normally curriculum-bound and oriented to current curricular offerings. Moreover, as opposed to public libraries, the clientele tends to be at least 18 years of age, and better educated than a corresponding group who patronize the community library. Written acquisition policies offer guidelines to assist the librarian or subject bibliographer in the selection of materials to meet stated primary and subsidiary functions of a particular library. Policies may be brief or lengthy, depending upon the degree of built-in flexibility or detail desired. Information on the acquisition and handling of serial publications may include a statement outlining policy for such tangible aspects as backsets, microform or duplicate copies, disposition of gifts and exchange material, and regulatory directives on levels of collection intensity within a given subject area. But more often than not, they may be mute on the issue of censorship in establishing an account of the responsibilities of collection development.

Academic library policies place an emphasis on providing materials to support staff and students in current teaching and research programs. Materials of general information in subject areas not covered by instructional and research programs or materials for recreational purposes may fall under a corollary function designation which, in fact, may be more akin to a fall by the wayside.[11] While faculty members are instrumental in keeping library personnel abreast of new or proposed research and degree programs and in offering recommendations for the acquisition of specific titles, the librarian carries the professional responsibility for building, balancing, and managing the collection and coordinating the resource development of the library as a whole; and sometimes a fine line exists between de-selection and censorship.

So what happens in an academic library with an established serials acquisition policy, when a request for *Playboy, Penthouse,* or *Oui* crosses the desk of a bibliographer? Utilizing the criteria in the collection profile as the initial source of reference, the bibliographer must then make a qualitative judgment of the serial. Even in an institution where sex is designated a specific and/or serious area of psychological or sociological research, and in which scholarly-oriented journals are conscientiously or even aggressively acquired, the justification for acquiring these three magazines, or others similar in nature, may present a problem. Escalating costs and space limitations prohibit acquisition of all publications in a given area, and each title must be judged on its individual merits. Quality of textual or illustrative material, format and presentation, level of interest, and permanent value to the collection are all considered. The library's budget is influential in a decision as well, for the acquisition of any serial publication represents an ongoing financial commitment.

The difficulty with controversial materials in academic libraries is that they are often short-lived and trendy; and bibliographers, based on their experience with journals which have folded in the past, may decide to postpone an initial investment until a publication has established a safe niche for itself in the publishing world or consumer market. This presents no problem for *Playboy* or *Penthouse,* however, both of which enjoy millions of subscriptions, a longstanding history, and major advertising revenue. If the publication is indexed, the demand for it may increase, and a bibliographer's predisposition may be positively influenced. Unless a library's collection profile emphasizes erotica or contains a special collection of sexually-oriented material, based upon previous collection-development decisions, titles which do not serve an immediate educational purpose, or are not considered organic to the dynamics of present growth, do not find an easy path to the shelf. In many cases, it is easier to justify the non-selection of controversial material than its selection, which is only one of the points of similarity between academic and public libraries.

Academic libraries, like public libraries, are not immune to internal or external political pressure. Bibliographers are accountable for their decisions to their supervisors, and the library in a state-supported institution is dependent upon the legislature for a large amount of its funding. Once a decision is made to place controversial material in the library, the individuals responsible, or the institution involved, may be called upon to defend its inclusion, and may, in so doing, open themselves to a barrage of attacks from partisan groups which often exert pressure to remove challenged items.

The *Tallahassee Democrat* for June 30, 1977[12] reported that Florida's Governor Askew had vetoed a bill which would have set up censorship committees in state colleges and universities. Askew roundly criticized the faculty of the University of West Florida at Pensacola for showing the film *Deep Throat*, even though students were not required to attend. He contended that the taxpayers "have a right to expect better" from state schools, while maintaining, to his credit, in the same veto message, that "Government must act with restraint in considering the measures which touch upon the academic atmosphere of a university." In effect, what Askew was doing comes close to what librarians must do under similar circumstances. They must be careful to distinguish between criticism and suppression. In the case mentioned, the university escaped front-line battle with the legislature, but librarians must be prepared for the various assaults or attempts which may be directed toward the suppression of library material, for whatever reason, and from whatever faction. Censorship, in its various forms, is neither new nor in the process of fading into oblivion in academic libraries.

D. H. Lawrence spoke of what he called the "censor-morons" who plagued him from the beginning of his career. In 1928, the year in which Lawrence began to bombard English-speaking countries with the Florentine edition of his *Lady Chatterley's Lover*, he wrote to Morris Ernst, in an acknowledgement of Ernst's book *To the Pure:*

Our civilization cannot afford to let the censor-moron loose. The censor-moron does not really hate anything but the living and growing human consciousness. It is our developing and extending consciousness that he threatens—and our consciousness in its newest, most sensitive activity, its vital growth. To arrest or circumscribe the vital consciousness is to produce morons, and nothing but a moron would do it.[13]

Whether the censor-morons surface in a state legislature or in partisan women's groups which attempt to suppress material that they consider exploitive or harmful to their cause, *Playboy, Penthouse,* and *Oui,* once acquired for a library's collection, should be made available to any reader if the library is to cultivate a sense of integrity as a source of information and a promoter of free inquiry. This is a signal difference between public and academic libraries, as, in public libraries, an occasional compromise is permissible, to shield the young and/or to get the belligerent watchdogs off our backs. In academic libraries, it is essential that all who seek information, knowledge, or entertainment be given untrammeled access to it, as an axiomatic tenet of a free educational system.

Sexism, as well as racism, anti-Semitism, or any other ism, will not be eliminated from our culture by removing certain titles from library shelves. Information on feminist ideology as well as material written to challenge old values and extol the new can be made available on library shelves, right next to *Playboy,* for the user to select, reject, or ignore. The Miltonian belief that, if presented with all the facts, an individual can and will make intelligent, wise decisions, presupposes a belief in the basic goodness of people and faith in their ability and judgment. And if librarians are asked daily to resolve the dichotomy between information needs and budgetary and selection restraints, hopefully, in attempting to do so, we can at least remain alert and sensitive to the underlying problems.

Ordering

Although much of the wide variety of men's magazines available across the counter at an adult bookstore remains elusive to an acquisitions librarian through ordinary channels of acquisition, *Playboy, Penthouse,* and *Oui* present no problem. All are available through direct subscription and are listed in the catalogs of various subscription agencies. These more "sophisticated" magazines enjoy international readership, have found their way into local supermarket magazine racks as well as adult bookstores, and are as accessible as bread or tea, *Time* or *Newsweek.* They are also dependable from a librarian's point of view, as each is published monthly and, once an order has been placed and paid for, a librarian can be fairly certain that the issues will arrive consistently and predictably, with adherence to the publication schedule. An inherent danger in subscribing to one or more of the lesser-known titles (which are not indexed, anyway) is the potential instability of the magazine. Premature cessation, irregular receipt of issues, non-receipt of issues, long delays, improper or incorrect address labeling, can and do contribute to problems for the serials librarian. Claims generated for missing issues and letters requesting information on publication status are time-consuming and costly. Any additional staff time spent on handling, processing, or incidentally claiming wayward issues, quickly increases the overall cost of a publication to a library, despite a possible low initial investment. When this happens repeatedly with unsatisfactory results or responses, a librarian may decide that cancelling a subscription is preferable to hassling with it every month.

Cataloging and Classification

The Library of Congress has classified *Playboy, Penthouse,* and *Oui* under its 'general works' heading, AP2, for periodicals in English published in the United States. This places them in the same classification with all other magazines of universal scope. The sexual content or representation is not singled out as the predominant or basic characteristic. To identify or emphasize the erotic nature of a magazine in a collection, the HQ section of the LC classification, dealing with "Social Groups, the Family, Marriage, Woman" (although in need of an extensive overhaul) offers alternatives. Erotic material of a periodical nature is placed under HQ450. The HQ section also provides a classification for works for special sex and age groups. HQ36 is specifically for men. The classification number assigned to a men's magazine for any individual library will depend on that library's reasons for adding that specific title to the collection. Although each title is handled and cataloged separately, it must be integrated into an existing collection and be consistent with current collection development practices.

Subject access points may be non-existent if the title has been placed in a general works classification. If attention is to be drawn to the erotic, photographic, or literary aspects of the publication, then some form of subject access is required. Applicable Library of Congress subject headings would include: Art and morals; Erotica; Erotic art; Erotic Literature; Nude in Art; Photography, Artistic; Photography, Erotic; Photography of the nude; Photography of women; Sex in literature; and, yes, Pornography.

Location and User Access

Once a decision is made to subscribe to a controversial title, a librarian must consider the alternatives and options available in determining its location in the collection, and the effect that decision will have on overall accessibility. Like book and magazine sellers who may choose to shelve material with sexual content on high racks, or behind counters where they must be requested for perusal or purchase, librarians may elect to place their titles in some form of limited access area, but not, as it may be argued, to protect the reader from the title, but rather to protect the title from the reader. This is more true, of course, in academic library situations, where all readers are presumed to be adult, than it may be in public libraries, where the young, the innocent, and the susceptible find such titles at times the forbidden fruit of the fable. If a title survives de-selection, tight budgets, and the censor-morons, the last and greatest threat to its survival and shelf-life may come from the patron.

Issues which mysteriously (or systematically) disappear from open shelves, or which turn up mutilated with only an open staple where the centerfold once reposed, are no longer available for use by other readers. Empty shelves or spotty and unreliable holdings do not foster trust in the ability of the collection to produce what it purports to have acquired. Because repeated and necessary replacement of missing issues constitutes an additional expense per title for the library, titles that are in high demand or issues frequently mutilated or missing from the shelves may require special protective custody. Ideally, a sophisticated security system will eliminate outright theft, but special handling often is necessary or desirable, nonetheless.

Alternatives to open shelving range from minimum to maximum security levels. Titles may be placed in a special collections area, a reserve area, behind a designated desk, or locked in an area where they are available on demand, through appropriate channels. As long as a title and its location are listed in the library's catalog, it can be found by anyone searching the records of the library's holdings. But anyone browsing the open shelving section in a library which enforces protective measures for a periodical title (or a whole class of titles) will miss those items which are shelved elsewhere.

If *Playboy, Penthouse,* and *Oui* are shelved behind a desk or in a special location where they must be requested directly from library personnel, the possibility exists that certain patrons may be intimidated and will not venture forth to risk a face-to-face confrontation for something which would cause no embarrassment if placed on open shelving. This is an example of a well-known legal concept: the chilling effect. Problems arise when a patron is asked to leave an identification card and sign a name and address in order to check out a periodical issue. At one midwestern university library, a patron declined receipt of the issue he had requested when he realized that he would have to sign his name in order to check it out; in another instance, a patron who had signed out an issue of *Playboy* returned the issue, requested the check-out card, and completely obliterated his signature with many dark strokes of a black pen.

One possible alternative to tight security measures for print copies of these titles is in the acquisition and retention of a back file on microform. The trend toward microform acquisition of publications in libraries has been precipitated in part by escalating costs of subscriptions and binding, shrinking budgetary allocations and shelf-space. Another equally important contributing factor is the reluctant conclusion on the part of all librarians that the honor system just doesn't work, and that prudent security is necessary. Microforms as a backup for high-theft, high-mutilation titles is highly desirable, when replacement costs cut into limited acquisitions funding. Although microform copies in the collection may resolve some of the difficulties which arise when material must be guarded and kept, there is noticeable patron resistance to them, and obvious shortcomings when photographic material is the sought item. Microforms, however, are becoming the only expedient way that libraries can make materials freely available and, at the same time, be reasonably certain that they will be returned after use.

LOOKING AHEAD: SEX MAGAZINES, CENSORSHIP, AND THE NEW TECHNOLOGY

Futuring is, by definition, an imprecise science, and that's what makes it so much fun. That no one can predict, with any degree of precision, that which is yet to come, is a truism, but it is still often profitable to do a little crystal-ball gazing, to attempt to speculate about what awaits us so that we may be ready for it, remembering always that predictions, projections and prophecies may be, and usually are, wrong. So here are the authors' scenarios of some likely eventualities for sex magazines in libraries. They are alternative futures with which you are free to disagree. As a matter of fact, if you have other, better, ideas, the authors would welcome a look at them. With the understanding, then, that this is a very tricky thing to attempt, we push these conjectures and scenarios hesitantly forward for your inspection.

As far as libraries go, the most important feature of subscriptions to magazines in the future will be cost, rather than what is printed or displayed in them. It is demonstrable that, almost everywhere, library budgets cannot keep pace with materials costs, which occasions the following scene increasingly in public and academic libraries: A routing sheet makes the rounds with the complete list of serials holdings and a stern directive from "topside" that each person addressed is to indicate all titles he or she thinks "the library could live without." Agonizing decisions are called for, but increasing pressure falls upon libraries to "do without" expensive and recreational magazines, a category which encompasses *Playboy, Penthouse,* and *Oui.* Donations of issues solve the problem of original cost, but create other costly problems, if the titles are to be officially accessioned for the collection.

Three other factors loom on the horizon for libraries. *Microforms,* as has been previously discussed, obviate some of the cost and theft problems, but meet, at present, with sales resistance from the library's public. The future will bring improvements in hardware and software as regards microforms, which, together with growing acceptance of their existence and use, may result in the continuation of subscriptions despite inflation and shrinking budgets. Computerized *on-line journals* are intriguing, as the reader is free to order up only that which he or she wishes to read, leaving the rest in the system. In this way, easily-offended persons will not find themselves confronting full-color illustrations of things they'd just as soon not see, and parents will be able to assume supervisory responsibility for that which their own children may order. Finally, *publication on demand* may permeate the magazine industry, essentially leaving libraries out of the transaction. Since a single copy of a magazine now has the potentiality of serving a limitless number of users, individual and tailored magazines, available through the mails, or via one's personal home information/entertainment system, will take some promotion before the public is ready for them.

Changing tastes in our society might render such magazines as *Playboy* and its genre totally non-controversial. The direction moved in by popular tastes and attitudes could be one way or the other, but these scenarios represent some of the fascinating possibilities:

Scenario A: Societal Change. Sex magazines continue as they are, showing female nudity and related thematic material, but nobody much cares. Challenges and objections diminish or cease altogether because television, movies, and live entertainment have gone substantially beyond mere two-dimensional representations of naked females. Those who today inveigh against the undraped female body spread across three pages in their magazines may have other things to worry about by the year 2000. A more permissive society, an anything-goes attitude among youth, and a spreading belief that sex is an important part of life, to be enjoyed and discussed openly, rather than repressed and mysterious, may pervade our national consciousness, leaving *Playboy* and its competitors tame by comparison with alternative entertainments.

Scenario B: Playboy's End. Such magazines as *Playboy, Penthouse,* and *Oui* will no longer trouble libraries or their patrons in a few decades, because they will no longer exist. By the year 2000, the world's economy may have undergone such cataclysmic changes that expensive and sophisticated slick magazines, always escalating in price, have priced themselves out of the market. In a world where most of us will have to hustle to insure meat on the table and shelter for the night, such luxuries as magazines, especially those not dedicated to telling us how to squeeze more from our shrinking dollars, will expire quietly, with no swan song, no funeral, and no tomb.

Scenario C: Exit the Library. Playboy and the others may or may not exist in the future, but it won't be a library problem, because the library will no longer exist. Commercial availability of entertainment and services going far beyond our present efforts to serve the community, coupled with a public feeling that the library is a growing drain on our stretched-to-the-limits property-tax dollars, will sink the library. Perhaps the library will mutate into something else, such as a bookstore/record store/lending library, or an experience parlor, where holograms are experienced, not viewed or read, or even perhaps a burned-out shell of a building, charred to cinders in some stupid global war. Depressing? Sure, but we really can't rule it out, can we?

Scenario D: Editorial Change. The magazines will still exist and be bought by libraries, but, due to decisions financial, moral, or based on market analysis, the content of today's sex magazines will be metamorphosized into a more widely acceptable incarnation. It is possible that a wave of revivalism will sweep this troubled land, and it will become a reprehensible act to look at, or even want to look at, "nekkid ladies." Publishers will be born again, repent of their youthful follies, and will recast their magazines such that they reflect traditional values: respect for womanhood and love for the flag. The pornographer will be forced to see that there is no money in his wares, and will, voluntarily or otherwise, be put out of business. Sexuality will be criminally or morally reprehensible, and some Ayatollah-like leader of vision and charisma will indignantly condemn the acquisition by libraries or display or retention of whatever is still being sold.

One final scenario, which may be the most likely of all, runs along the general lines of *status quo*. The same libraries (or different ones) will have the same problems with the same kinds of patrons, and all the high drama of censorship cases will repeat itself endlessly across the decades.

With that exception, however, the scenarios we have drawn all point to one optimistic conclusion: for whatever reasons, and under whatever circumstances, there will be no (or damn near no) hassles for libraries over *Playboy, Penthouse,* or *Oui.* This may or may not be cause for celebration, as the reason for the dwindling problems of this nature may be the demise of the magazines, of the libraries, or of the society itself. But one way or another, we predict boldly that based on rational speculation about the future, the present problems libraries have with such magazines are temporary, and will shortly (as time is measured) disappear. For the time being, however, the dilemma of the public or academic librarian confronted by such problems will continue to be very real indeed. Even so, it should be remembered that we are not passive or helpless onlookers as we watch library history unfold. Each of us has the ability to influence decisions today which will make tomorrow turn out differently—for better or for worse, who can say? We can try to shape a future of our choosing, and a world where libraries may buy and make available with complete freedom *anything* which their audiences request, appreciate, or need.

REFERENCES

1. Rossi, Lee D., "The Whore vs. the Girl Next Door: Stereotypes of Women in *Playboy, Penthouse* and *Oui.*" *Journal of Popular Culture* 9 (Summer, 1975):90-94.
2. U. S. 5th Circuit Court of Appeals. Court Case: *Penthouse, International vs. McAuliffe* (now being tried, Summer, 1979).
3. Fiske, Marjorie, *Book Selection and Censorship: A Study of School and Public Libraries in California* (Berkeley: University of California Press, 1959).
4. Busha, Charles, *Freedom vs. Supression and Censorship* (Littleton, Colorado: Libraries, Unlimited, 1972).
5. Oboler, Eli M., *The Fear of the Word: Censorship and Sex* (Metuchen, N.J.: Scarecrow Press, 1974).
6. Liston, Robert A., *The Right to Know: Censorship in America* (New York: Franklin Watts, Inc., 1973).
7. Daily, Jay E., *An Anatomy of Censorship* (New York: Marcel Dekker, Inc., 1973), 254.
8. *op. cit.,* 256.
9. *op. cit.,* 263.
10. Van den Haag, Ernest, "The Case for Pornography is the Case for Censorship and Vice Versa." *Esquire* (May, 1967):134-135.
11. See: Futas, Elizabeth, ed. *Library Acquisition Policies and Procedures* (Phoenix, AZ, Oryx Press, 1977) for an examination of 26 full-text policies covering print and non-print materials, as well as acquisition information from 300 academic and public libraries.
12. "Censorship Bill Vetoes." *Tallahassee Democrat,* 30 June 1977, sec. 4, p. 37.
13. Lawrence, D. H., *Sex, Literature and Censorship* (New York: Viking Press 1959), 9.

TREATMENT OF SEXUALLY ORIENTED MAGAZINES BY LIBRARIES

Roy M. Mersky
Michael L. Richmond

This article does not attempt to treat an ultimate issue: should libraries make the effort to collect obscene material. Rather, assuming the answer to be positive, it considers the problems which may face the librarian who has made the decision and proposes possible solutions. The initial selection determination should be governed by sound principles of the profession, all of which in some way or other return to the basic: "Select the right books for the library's readers."[1] If the legitimate educational or scientific ends of the patrons require the collection of pornographic material, then the librarian must face the knotty problem of placing it in the collection.

A more difficult problem exists in simply defining terms. The Supreme Court of the United States has been wrestling with the problem for years now, yet still has not derived a satisfactory formula. One justice, perhaps out of frustration with the Court's efforts, admitted his inability to define obscenity, but felt he was perfectly able to know it when he saw it.[2] Initially, the Supreme Court felt it had done its duty by defining as obscene, ". . . material which deals with sex in a manner appealing to prurient interest."[3] Over the ensuing years, this test proved increasingly unworkable, so that the Court slowly evolved the present test:

> . . . *(a) whether the 'average person, applying contemporary community standards,' would find that the work, taken as a whole, appeals to the prurient interest; (b) whether the work depicts or describes, in a patently offensive way, sexual conduct specifically defined by the applicable state law; and (c) whether the work, taken as a whole, lacks serious literary, artistic, political, or scientific value.*[4]

Even this, the *Miller* test, continues to come under scrutiny and to be altered.[5]

We may, of course, agree with Bertrand Russell that "Obscenity is whatever happens to shock some elderly and ignorant magistrate."[6] For our purposes, however, the definition which serves best may well be the more pragmatic test: that which will subject the disseminator to criminal prosecution in absence of any claim of privilege. In other words, we will explore the problems and methodology of collecting material which other people would call pornographic.

The problems in developing a collection of this nature stem from two sources: the material itself, and outside pressures. The availability of "dirty magazines" poses a considerable hurdle. With the exception of a few selections in the field which have established a certain degree of legitimacy and a solid core of readers (*Playboy, Penthouse,* and a handful of others), these items come out irregularly and often disappear from the market within a few issues.[7] Subscriptions, although frequently available, must go to the publishers themselves, as these publishers often are unwilling to deal through jobbers.[8] Some of these items will change price from issue to issue, making bookkeeping at best difficult. Compounding all of these problems, the librarian can look forward to regular visits to the neighborhood "adult" bookstore and making purchases on a cash only basis.

Thus, the very acquisition of the material presents scores of problems from the ordering to the payment. Even the selection process is complicated. New offerings spring up on the scene with the rapidity of the dragon's-teeth soldiers which menaced the Argonauts. Even assuming the capability to identify all of the magazines which comprise the universe from which the librarian is to select, identification of their contents frequently cannot be made. Such promotional material as may be available gives little guidance; most simply speaks in general terms of the sensual qualities of the photographs and prose. The tactic of visiting the local bookstore will bear little fruit, for most magazines of this nature are sealed to discourage browsing. Hence, all that can be seen of these items are the front and rear covers.

How can the librarian collecting in the area surmount these problems? In the case of the established dozen or so magazines which cater to this clientele, subscriptions will be readily available and the other problems will also be minimal.[9] If the collection is to be limited to these items, the librarian will be able to develop it with little more than the normal problems faced in making any serial acquisition. Indeed, this acquisition policy will avoid most of the problems to be discussed herein, simply given the established nature of the periodicals. On the other hand, materials of a more "hard-core" bent will not come so easily. In their case, the librarian may encounter a friendly bookseller, who will permit inspection of the interior of the magazines before purchase, and who may even notify the librarian when new materials arrive. Through such a source, the librarian can make contact with publishers and their representatives, thereby further simplifying the task.

On the whole, however, the librarian may find acquisitions difficulties so great that the nature of the collection becomes dictated by the availability of material. As with all things, the return gained for the cost expended must reasonably balance. The time and effort may increase the cost of a single volume to $50 or more, and at this point the librarian must call a halt.

All aspects of technical services will be affected by such a program. In addition to the problems of acquisitions, magnified in a state system by the expenditure of state funds on items which many voters deem improper, cataloging will find itself at wit's end trying to decipher the problems occasioned by this material. Some of the magazines contain only photographs; some have text dispersed throughout. Format changes will plague serials and cataloging departments alike, which will have to change records on an annoyingly frequent basis. The physical quality of the material will make binding very difficult, for margins are often ignored, and if one binds a centerfold one may eliminate considerable portions of the subject's anatomy. The paper used in many of these magazines will not stand up to binding, and may disintegrate in a matter of years. While these physical problems can be surmounted by modern microfilming techniques, other departments will be forced to improvise to adapt themselves to the new material. Little can be done to make regular that which is by its very nature irregular; the cataloging and serials librarians will simply have to try to adapt their existing systems. Alternatively, a separate portion of the collection could be designated for these items, with its own cataloging and indexing systems. True, this fragmentation of collections meets with disfavor in many cases, but is recognized as necessary in many others. Given the difficult nature of this material, combined with the need to house it in a controlled area apart from the rest of the collection,[10] this separate treatment may well be the answer.[11]

A problem of a slightly different nature occurs simply in the transmission of the material from the publisher to the library. Federal statutes prohibit both the use of the mails to disseminate obscene materials[12] and the importation of obscene material.[13] A body of cases, however, arose to permit libraries to procure this material in certain instances. Before the development of the test in *Roth*,[14] federal courts were permitting obscene material to be imported and sent through the mail, based on the theory of conditional privilege, when used to further ". . . scientific research and education."[15] Subsequent to *Roth*, deviations from the hard rules of the statutes were permitted on the ground that

. . . it is the importer's scientific interest in the material which leads to the conditional privilege, and it is this same interest which requires the holding that the appeal of the material to the scientist is not to his prurient interest and that, therefore, the material is not obscene as to him.[16]

There has been concern, however, that the new test promulgated in *Miller*[17] may have changed the theoretical underpinnings of the exceptions so they no longer exist. The requirement noted earlier that "contemporary community standards" be used to determine the "prurient interest" of a work may mean courts will no longer consider whether work is prurient as to an individual. In a case decided shortly after *Miller*, Mr. Justice Douglas noted in his dissent that:

> *Every author, every bookseller, every movie exhibitor, and perhaps, every librarian is now at the mercy of the local police force's conception of what appeals to the 'prurient interest' or is 'patently offensive.' The standards can vary from town to town and day to day in an unpredictable fashion.*[18]

It is true that the *Miller* test requires that an item not have serious scientific value before sanctions against obscenity will apply.[19] Set against this, however, have been the concerns of Justice Douglas[20] and representatives of library science educators, the American Booksellers Association, and the American Library Association.[21]

Simply stated, the librarian collecting in this area must do so courageously. There may well be serious legal ramifications to acquiring some of this material, and the library's legal counsel should be consulted. In any event, precautions should be taken in the dissemination of this material to avoid other legal problems.

Whether the *Miller* test will permit collection of sexually oriented materials has little bearing on their dissemination. In any event, these materials can be secured only for valid educational or scientific purposes. Any other use would be illegal. Complying with this requirement will create additional expense for any collecting library, for controls must be exercised similar to those in a rare book collection.

> *While there are some separate buildings housing extensive rare book collections, only the largest and wealthiest institutions can afford such a luxury, and even a separate room in the library with a full- or part-time attendant is beyond the means of most colleges. The most practical substitute is a section of the stacks that has been screened off, or even a bookcase with a glass or wire screen door that locks .... There should be provision, of course, for qualified readers to work with such a collection ....*[22]

The housing of the collection presents only the smallest problem. Controlled access is the rule for this collection, for central to the avoidance of litigation is the purpose for which access is given. Granted that librarians may demur at inquiring of a patron's purpose in using materials on principles of intellectual freedom, the Association of Research Libraries has long recognized that in certain instances such inquiry may be necessary. "Librarians should give all *qualified* investigators complete freedom of access to manuscripts."[23] Thus, it would be entirely proper for a librarian to require a patron to complete a form indicating name, supporting organization, nature and purpose of research, and similar data. Letters of introduction from faculty could also be required.

The mechanics of controlling patron access will mean additional expense for the library. Even if nothing more be done than the simple act of having the patron complete a form, reviewing the form, and giving the patron access to a closed room, the time of a librarian is consumed. The very forms themselves represent an additional cost. If the room housing the collection is attended, the salary of the attendant becomes yet another factor.

Other problems exist as well. To what extent will the materials be sent out on interlibrary loan? Will any part of the collection circulate to regular patrons? Will access within the closed area be direct, or will the patron require the services of a staff member to get the material?

For many years, the Library of Congress maintained the "Delta Collection" of obscene material collected by federal agents as exhibits in prosecutions. This collection has been abandoned. In the early 1960s, publicity and changing concepts of obscenity caused the materials in the collection to be dispersed throughout the general collection. Today, just a trickle of obscene material enters the Library of Congress, which feels no historical responsibility for collecting aggressively in this area, given the excellent collection maintained by the Institute for Sex Research at Indiana University.[24]

In this light, librarians contemplating collections of sexually oriented magazines should seriously consider the scope of their proposed holdings. By all means, if patron need exists the library should attempt to surmount the obstacles to acquisition and maintenance of such a collection. However, the path to be travelled is fraught with problems. The librarian must learn of their existence and be prepared to counter them. Courage is the handmaiden of the library profession, for librarians have battled bluenoses since the first book was collected. Courts uphold the rights of libraries to collect material regularly, even when the material is erotic in nature and has been placed in a high school collection.[25] Librarians must uphold the rights of their patrons to have access to materials supportive of their research.

Whether or not the librarian decides to collect obscene material, the decision should not rest on the propriety of pornography.

An actual or theoretical obscenity quotient is not a criterion of selection. Neither Haines, nor Carter and Bonk, nor Ranganathan mention it. The librarian who rejects Valley of the Dolls *or* The Arrangement *as trash is on firm literary ground; the librarian who rejects either because of its sexual content must in consistency withdraw a host of much better books from his collection.*[26]

REFERENCES

[1] M. Carter & W. Bonk, *Building Library Collections* 15 (1964).
[2] *Jacobellis v. Ohio*, 378 U.S. 184, 197 (1964, Stewart, J., concurring).
[3] *Roth v. United States*, 354 U.S. 476, 489 (1957).
[4] *Miller v. California*, 413 U.S. 15, 24 (1973).
[5] *Paris Adult Theater I v. Slaton*, 413 U.S. 49 (1973). See also L. Merritt, *Book Selection and Intellectual Freedom* 13 (1970).
[6] Attributed to Bertrand Russell. J. Simpson, ed., *Contemporary Quotations* 55 (1964).
[7] For example *Adam Film World*, a magazine of apparently limited availability, published 11 issues during one year, 9 issues the next, and 6 the year following. In contrast, *Playboy* has consistently published 12 regular issues since its inception.
[8] "If a library ordered a book from us which we definitely knew was pornographic, we would advise the library that the book was not available through us." Letter from Paul A. Rothman to Michael Richmond, dated August 1, 1979.
[9] See note 7, *supra*.
[10] See discussion *infra* accompanying note 21.

[11] For more specific suggestions on establishing a special collection, see generally R. Rogers & D. Weber, *University Library Administration* (1971) at 247 *et seq.*
[12] 18 U.S.C. §1461 (1976).
[13] 19 U.S.C. §1305(a) (1976).
[14] See note 3, *supra.*
[15] *Parmalee v. United States,* 113 F.2d 729, 737 (D.C. Cir. 1940); *United States v. Rebhuhn,* 109 F.2d 512 (2d Cir. 1940).
[16] *United States v. 31 Photographs,* 156 F. Supp. 350, 358 (S.D.N.Y. 1957). See also *United States v. One Unbound Volume,* 128 F. Supp. 280 (D. Md. 1955).
[17] See note 4, *supra.*
[18] *Trinkler v. Alabama,* 414 U.S. 955, 957 (1973) (Douglas, J., dissenting).
[19] *Miller* at 24.
[20] *Paris Adult Theatre I* at 71 (Douglas, J., dissenting).
[21] *Trinkler* at 957, n. 4.
[22] G. Lyle, *The Administration of the College Library* 286 (1961).
[23] Association of Research Libraries, *Report of the Committee on the Use of Manuscripts by Visiting Scholars,* in ARL *Minutes* 32 (July 6-7, 1951) (emphasis supplied).
[24] Telephone conversation between William Matheson and Michael Richmond, May 14, 1979.
[25] *Right to Read Defense Committee v. School Committee,* 454 F. Supp. 703 (D. Mass. 1978).
[26] *Merritt* at 14.

SEX, SERIALS AND THE LAW

Richard C. Dahl

I have always felt one could at any time write an article entitled " *'Something'* and the Law." Law cuts across all disciplines one way or another, and there are thousands of cases dealing with almost an infinity of subjects. When asked if I could come up with a brief article dealing with Sex, Serials and the Law, I thought it would be easy. I was wrong.

As a lawyer, I know where to find the law; as a librarian, I know serials are not something you eat for breakfast; and as a human, sex is more than a passing interest of mine. So why hasn't it been easy to come up with a brief, hard-hitting article touching on these three areas?

Certainly there have been some problems connected with sex and serials in libraries. My own experiences with these matters during the last 25 years, although few and only mildly traumatic, show that even a sheltered law librarian may encounter sex in the library.

About 20 years ago an army captain hurried into my library and asked me if I had anything on necrophilia. After I had sent him away with a book and two articles, my reference librarian, a maiden lady of uncertain age, who had overheard the request, asked me what necrophilia was. After explaining with my usual delicacy that this involved the misuse of a dead body, she looked at me and said, "Oh, Mr. Dahl, were they married?"

Sex may not have changed but times certainly have and the mysteries of sex turn up frequently even in our popular magazines. *Good Housekeeping* perhaps will not be doing an article on necrophilia, but I would not be surprised to learn that *Cosmopolitan* spends more time discussing orgasms than recipes for oatmeal cookies.

A second encounter I had with sex in the library that same year illustrates some of the changes that 20 years have brought about. A navy commander had told me he was assigned to rewrite navy regulations dealing with homosexuality. I told him that I had recently come across a case dealing with a magazine written for homosexuals, *One*, where the United States Supreme Court had reversed a lower court decision that held that the articles in the magazine were nothing more than cheap pornography, and it was therefore not mailable *(One, Inc. vs. Olesen,* 355 U.S. 371, Jan. 13, 1958). The commander asked that I get him some issues of the magazine. I told him I would get them on Interlibrary Loan from the Library of Congress, and later asked our reference librarian to do so. Several weeks later I got a call from the Library of Congress telling me that the homosexual magazine I wished to borrow was in their Delta Collection and that therefore I would have to pick it up in person. The next day I went over to the Library of Congress and entered the very large office that handled the circulation of materials to other federal libraries. I gave my name to the librarian at the desk and asked for the magazine. "Oh, yes, Mr. Dahl," she said in a loud and penetrating voice, "that homosexual magazine you want is in Mr. Obear's office." Unfortunately Mr. Obear's office was about 50 feet away, and I had to walk past about 30 interested employees. Today, I could have carried it off with perhaps some style; but, in those days before all those closets opened and gay liberation flowered, we male librarians felt somewhat suspect, like hairdressers or interior decorators. Thus, the walk to Mr. Obear's office seemed to take forever.

Actually, by today's standards, *One* magazine was quite mild and inoffensive, filled with interesting advertisements for moonglo pajamas and articles about how to meet friends in Denmark. In contrast, in preparation for this article, I bought and read an issue of *Hustler*, a magazine that was on trial for obscenity in Atlanta last spring. *Hustler* is the sort of magazine that gives pornography a bad name. I suppose that some persons might find the material prurient, a word that I have a hard time pronouncing, much less spelling, but I personally found it about as exciting as an unwashed sock. I suppose that my problem is that I cannot be both excited and nauseated at the same time. However, I suspect that one man's meat is another man's pornography. I learned this some years ago when I came across several issues of a magazine named *Bizarre*. Someone had donated several issues of this magazine to our library along with a stack of old law reviews. *Bizarre* catered to readers with very odd taste, most of whom seemed to be in love with raincoats, high-heeled shoes, and an occasional vacuum cleaner.

I have touched on my three experiences with sex and serials in the library to make a couple of small points. I think these three magazines illustrate some of the tough problems the court must deal with in the area of pornography. It might not be too difficult to decide that these serials lack serious literary merit. Certainly, anyone with taste would say they are bad literature; but, are they obscene and pornographic? Thirty years ago this was no problem. In those days the air was clean and sex was dirty. Today, most courts find it difficult to define obscenity as its meaning is a relative and subjective one. Some feel that the definition of obscenity can never be clarified and must be a matter of opinion. In an ordinary criminal trial, everyone would agree that the crime (murder, rape, arson, theft, etc.) is reprehensible. The question to be decided is whether the accused did it. In an obscenity trial, however, it is usually admitted that the accused sold, displayed or distributed the publication, but the question is whether the action is reprehensible. The court, therefore, has to apply or formulate a workable censoring test to be used to identify that which is to be proscribed. In drafting a definition of obscenity or pornography, the law must be concerned with a balance between competing values. Social scientists, libertarians, persons with very strong religious feelings, and dirty old men will all exhibit a variety of views. In glancing through the literature in an effort to convince myself that writing an article of this sort is an exercise in futility, I found literally hundreds of articles for and against the censorship of obscenity. There are even a few apologists for pornography. One librarian writing in an Indiana publication even claimed that as a library page he developed an interest in reading through sampling the items in the locked case.

While a great many librarians have experienced censorship problems, most of these incidents did not involve serials. There have, however, been some problems with a few serials such as *Playboy, Penthouse, Ms.*, and *Evergreen Review.* Some underground newspapers have been the targets of attacks and a budget cut threat in Minneapolis caused two underground newspapers to be restricted to adult use.

Feelings were often intense, and conflicts bitter (a censorship fight in Long Island produced a bumper sticker that read: "Support your local degenerate, vote yes on the library budget"). Librarians, however, particularly serials librarians, are usually not the targets of legal prosecution. Most censorship incidents dealing with serials are settled one way or another before they end up as appellate court cases, where they would be setting legal precedents for the future. Thus, there is no case law specifically dealing with the problems of the serials librarian and censorship for sexual reasons.

There are, of course, hundreds of cases that deal with obscenity and pornography in other contexts. Some of what they say, if they would only say it clearly and consistently, would be relevant for the serials librarian faced with a censorship problem. Unfortunately, the obscenity cases that are dealt with in the courts are likely to encourage the serious danger of self-censorship, at least by those who feel they would not be comfortable as defendants in criminal cases.

Not only are there too many obscenity cases to be dealt with in a short article, there are too many statutes and local ordinances. Furthermore, if you wish to survey secondary authorities, there are hundreds of books and thousands of articles which may be relevant. A hurried survey of my law library produced a list of more than 100 law review articles written since the U.S. Supreme Court's new obscenity guidelines issued in *Miller vs. Calif.*, 413 U.S. 15 (1973). Also, it might be argued that the court in dismissing a nationwide standard and in ruling that "community standards" are the measure for determining whether a work is "prurient," has impossibly fragmented the law as there are some 20,000 local jurisdictions in the United States. England, Canada, Australia, New Zealand, and a host of other countries have faced the same problem, and to ignore them would be a disservice to readers outside the U.S.

Besides the central issue of a precise definition of the term obscenity, there is the question of what evils obscenity legislation is intended to combat. Some ask, is the threat of pornography sufficient to warrant use of the police and judicial power for its suppression? A great many persons who do not support pornography are still particularly uneasy about bureaucratic censorship. Unfortunately, history shows that in the past there has been a great abuse of censorship. George Jacob Holyoke was imprisoned in Gloucester for six months for 26 words uttered in Cheltenham in 1842. In 1942, as an American soldier stationed in Cheltenham, I must have uttered 2,600 words equally as bad.

There are many persons who loathe the dehumanizing nature of pornography and feel that the obscene does more than merely offend. They find it a deceptive glorification of perverse and inhuman values. Some of their opponents admit pornography may be a growth industry and that it presents a distorted view of reality, but they doubt that it leads to violence. They feel that the would-be censors are suffering from pornophobia. One fed-up teacher writing in an English journal stated that as parents evidently are not so concerned about the obscene words their children read on the walls of their school building, she proposed that teachers tear out the pages containing dirty words and paste them on the restroom walls.

Unfortunately, the law has not been very successful in balancing the rights of free expression against the concern with the possible evil influence of obscenity and pornography. In fact, one has the feeling that the innate complexity of the problem has been increased by the recent rulings of the United States Supreme Court. Furthermore, the cases exhibit certain inconsistencies; for example, in *Stanley vs. Georgia*, 1969, the Supreme Court permits possession of obscene material in one's home; while in *U.S. vs. 37 photographs*, 1971, it permits customs to seize obscene matter from one's luggage when enroute to one's home.

I suspect most librarians would agree that they have chosen a profession that commits them to the principle of intellectual freedom, and certainly they do not wish to allow a lawyer to decide whether or not a serial is to be acquired for their library. They can perhaps best protect themselves through associations which would work for exemption clauses for libraries in local obscenity laws and develop policies and procedures for dealing with the various actions by self-appointed censors.

I suppose I could write an article on sex, serials and the law, but it would be as complex and muddled as the law it was written about. I would be writing about two of my favorite subjects and two out of three is not so bad. Furthermore, an article about sex when it's good is terrific, and when it's bad it's pretty good.

EROTIC MAGAZINES
AND THE LAW

Jerold Nelson

More than six years ago, in 1973, in a series of decisions popularly labeled the Miller decisions, the Supreme Court of the United States provided a new set of standards for the legal treatment of materials alleged to be obscene. In a marked departure from previous rulings, the Burger Court reinterpreted the test of community standards to be the "local" community and placed on the accused the burden of proving redeeming social value. It was widely predicted that the decisions would introduce an era of increased censorship. The purpose of this study is to test whether that prediction has come true with regard to a set of printed materials among the most likely to be affected by the activity of the censor, erotic magazines.

Erotic magazines can be defined as serial publications in which material concerning or intending to arouse sexual desire is prominent. It should be understood that the content that is potentially offensive in these materials is almost exclusively pictorial.

The principal source of data for this study has been the reports of censorship activity that are published in the *Newsletter on Intellectual Freedom*.[1] Data drawn from the *Newsletter* from mid-1973 to the end of 1978 were analyzed to identify the number and frequency of incidents involving erotic magazines, the kinds of action taken, and the chronological and geographical distribution of the incidents.

ANALYSIS

The *Newsletter on Intellectual Freedom* listed 117 incidents involving censorship of erotic magazines during the period from the Miller decisions to the end of 1978. There were a total of 135 references to 26 individual magazines.[2] Among the magazines cited more than ten times was *Playboy,* which was involved in 29 separate incidents. *Penthouse* had 28 citations, *Hustler* 16, and *Oui* 14 (see Figure 1). In addition, there were 51 citations to "sexually explicit magazines" not otherwise identified. Almost all of the reports were related to newsstand sales. Three referred to the circulation of magazines in prisons and three referred to cases of transmitting materials through the mails. No libraries were reported as being involved in censorship cases resulting from the possession of erotic magazines during the period of this study.[3]

About 75% of the incidents were directed at restricting access of adults to the materials in question. Of those situations that dealt specifically

FIGURE 1. List of Erotic Magazines Cited as Problems.

Playboy	29
Penthouse	28
Hustler	16
Oui	14
Playgirl	8
Gallery	6
Screw	6
Club	3
Viva	3
Dapper	2
Pub	2
Smut	2
Swank	2
Best of Hustler II	1
Chic	1
Climax	1
Erection	1
Genesis	1
Girls of Playboy II	1
Love Partners	1
Nugget	1
Penthouse Loving Couples	1
Playboy Love Games	1
Probe	1
Rogue	1
Stag	1
"Sexually Explicit Magazines" (no title)	51

with the "protection" of juveniles, the most common was the requirement that newsstands not display sexually provocative magazine covers where they would be visible to young people.

Approximately one-third of the reported incidents were convictions for selling "obscene" magazines. In those cases where penalties were specified, they ranged from the $500 fine levied against a newsdealer in Malden, Massachusetts for selling a copy of *Penthouse Magazine*, to the potential penalty of $65,000 in fines and a maximum sentence of 60 years faced by the publisher of *Screw* and *Smut* for mailing obscene materials into Kansas (in a decision that was subsequently overturned by an appellate court). The average sentence, even when the unusually stiff penalty of the Kansas case is excluded, was a fine of $7,500 and a jail term of seven years.

Approximately 10% of the incidents reported acquittals or reversed convictions. Nearly 25% were reports of ordinances that had been introduced to limit the availability of erotic magazines, but which did not cite specific prosecutions. More than 25% of the cases dealt with extralegal censorship, usually unchallenged. Some examples: a vendor "voluntarily" removes magazines from his shelves; a local police chief announces that the citizens of his community have "entrusted him to decide what is obscene"; the mayor of a large city bans certain magazines from being sold on city property; well-attended rallies urge those who are present to use political tactics to rid the area of "sexually explicit magazines."

When the data are analyzed across time, there were fewer incidents at the beginning and at the end of the period. The most active periods were 1975, with 30 incidents reported, 1976, with 21 incidents, and 1977, with 32 (see Figure 2). It is reasonable to assume that the relative inactivity in the period just after the Miller decisions can be explained by the need for state legislatures to revise statutes to conform with the Supreme Court's new standards.

It is not clear why incidents again decline at the end of the period. There are at least two alternative possibilities. It may be that prosecutors were not satisfied with the effectiveness of their efforts, and moved their attention to other areas where the conviction ratio is higher. Or it may be that the efforts of law enforcement officials and government prosecutors were sufficiently successful so that there is no longer a strong motivation to pursue the eradication of what is seen as a diminishing problem. The evidence does show that in the most recent period of 1977-1978, pro-censorship actions (prosecutions, convictions, and unsuccessful appeals) still outnumbered anti-censorship actions (aquittals and successful appeals) by almost three to one.

The geographical distribution of reported incidents reveals that a few

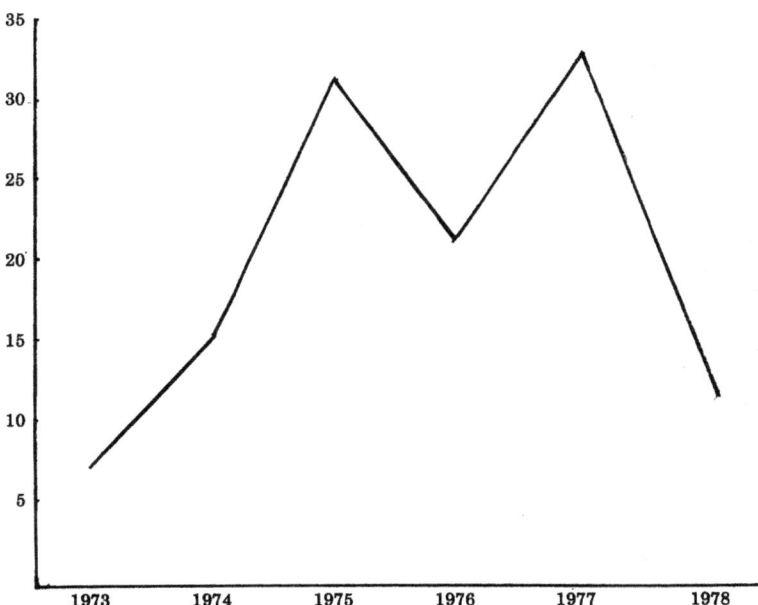

FIGURE 2. Frequency of Incidents Reported.

states have been very active in prosecuting erotic magazines while most states have been active in only a small way or not at all (Figure 3). There is no clearly defined "censorship belt." Ohio was cited most frequently with nine incidents, explained in part, perhaps, by the notoriety of the *Hustler* prosecution in that state. Michigan, Massachusetts, Texas, Georgia, Illinois, and New York were all the scene of at least five incidents. Since these states are also for the most part states with large populations, it may well be that much of the geographical variance can be explained by nothing more than population density. The most populous state, California, was the locus for three reported incidents. Twenty-six states were either involved in a single incident or had none at all.

CONCLUSIONS

The sheer number of censorship incidents involving erotic magazines, after a previous period of scant activity, suggests that the Miller decisions have had some impact in encouraging the prosecution of those who deal in such materials. A suggestion of diminished activity in the recent past may indicate that prosecution has not been sufficiently successful to warrant continued effort at the same level. It also may indicate that the effects of the earlier, higher level of attempted sup-

FIGURE 3. Incidents Reported by State.

State	Number of Incidents	State	Number of Incidents
Ohio	9	Connecticut	2
Michigan	8	Oregon	1
Massachusetts	6	District of Columbia	1
Texas	6	Alabama	1
Georgia	5	Idaho	1
Illinois	5	Mississippi	1
New York	5	Montana	1
Utah	4	Nebraska	1
Kansas	4	Nevada	1
Oklahoma	4	New Jersey	1
Virginia	4	North Carolina	1
New Hampshire	4	Rhode Island	1
Pennsylvania	4	South Carolina	1
California	3	Washington	1
Indiana	3	Wisconsin	1
Kentucky	3	Alaska	0
Maryland	3	Arizona	0
Tennessee	3	Arkansas	0
West Virginia	3	Colorado	0
Florida	3	Delaware	0
Iowa	3	Hawaii	0
Louisiana	3	Maine	0
Minnesota	2	New Mexico	0
Missouri	2	Wyoming	0
North Dakota	2	South Dakota	0
		Vermont	0

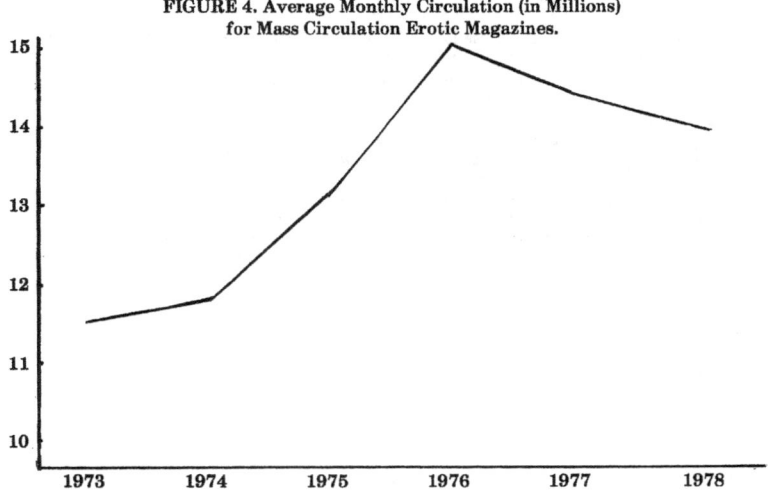

FIGURE 4. Average Monthly Circulation (in Millions) for Mass Circulation Erotic Magazines.

pression have kept traffic in objectionable materials within acceptable limits in those communities where local attitudes make their continued circulation a matter of concern. The circulation figures of the leading mass market erotic magazines were examined to see whether there had been a change in circulation that might provide some clue as to the effect of censorship efforts. Total monthly circulation is down about 8% from its peak in 1976,[4] but the change is not substantial enough to draw conclusions from it (Figure 4). The most that can be said is that circulation statistics do not refute the hypothesis that the Miller decisions have had an adverse effect on the availability of erotic magazines.

The reaction of some who have persisted in reading this far is undoubtedly "so what!" It is certainly true that few libraries hold even the mildest of the erotic magazines dealt with here.[5] At the other extreme, with the most explicit of the items, there are not many librarians who would be inclined to argue strenuously in favor of their continued existence, let alone advocate that libraries add them to their collections.

We are in possession of no positive evidence to suggest that censorship of erotic magazines has any effect, direct or indirect, on the freedom of libraries to provide appropriate periodicals for their customary clients. Nevertheless, those who are concerned with the health of intellectual freedom in this country will continue to believe that the diminution of freedom in any arena will diminish in some degree the freedom of all. The seeming growth of censorship in school libraries today may be an indication of the wisdom of such an attitude. At the very least, the situation described in this study warrants continued monitoring, and could in fact benefit from more intensive examination.

REFERENCES

1. *Newsletter on Intellectual Freedom.* Office of Intellectual Freedom, American Library Association. July, 1973-November, 1978.
2. The discrepancy between the number of references to magazines and the total number of incidents is explained by the fact that some incidents involved more than one magazine.
3. There were a number of incidents, however, in which issues of titles like *Time, Newsweek, Mademoiselle,* and *Cosmopolitan* were purged from school libraries for allegedly offensive erotic content.
4. Circulation figures courtesy of the publishers.
5. An examination of union periodical catalogs held by the Pacific Northwest Bibliographic Center indicated that only two of the region's largest library systems held anything but *Playboy,* and even *Playboy* was held by only a small minority of reporting libraries.

CHILDREN'S RIGHTS IN THE LIBRARY: A PERSONAL VIEW

Cynthia R. Howe

To see or not to see; to read or not to read, that is the question. Or, in more contemporary terms, how much or how little do we want to expose our children to sexual reading materials, and what is the public library's role in doing this? As a mother of two young children, what is my role in introducing my children to this form of literature? These are questions which need to be explored when one discusses children's rights in relation to sexual literature.

In discussing the public library's role in the issue, I think one must first define what function a public library serves in a community. I agree with the Library Bill of Rights that a library is "an institution of education for democratic living,"[1] which should strive to present all points of view to all people in that community. This is a big order, but ideally the public library should, in my opinion, serve the citizens of its community in an educational manner.

On this premise, I think one then must define what sexual materials would be acceptable for a library to carry in its children's section. If a library is to serve as an educational institution, then, in my mind, a magazine or book which deals with sexual subjects in a mature, responsible, educational manner would be acceptable in a library. On the other hand, sexual materials which are inaccurate, aim solely at arousal, or are obscene, either in language or pictorial presentation, would not be classified as "educational" and would not be suitable.

This description, I realize, is cursory at best, and is cause for debate. What may arouse one child may not arouse another; what is considered lewd or obscene language by one parent or library may be perfectly acceptable to another. Still, I think there is a definite line between educational sexual materials and pornography which most people realize. As Supreme Court Justice Potter Stewart said during an obscenity case in 1964, he found it hard to make an accurate verbal description of hard-core pornography, but, "I know it when I see it."[2] Isn't that true of most of us?

The second problem in discussing the library's role in dealing with children's sexual literature is defining the age at which one considers a child to be a child, and a young adult to be a young adult, and what kind of literature should be available to each. The lower age spectrum is relatively simple to classify. In my opinion, the young child might be classified between the ages of 4-9 years. Reading materials are simple and primarily pictorial. Sexual materials for the young child might include physical differences between the sexes and the human reproductive process (most children of this age group are experiencing pregnant mothers and new baby sisters or brothers).

The upper age spectrum is much more difficult to define because of the difference in rate at which a child matures mentally and physically. This has caused much discussion among school professionals and librarians.

In my opinion, the "young adult" classification might range between 10-15 years. When a person reaches 16, he/she often is given the responsibility of driving a car, holding a job, or running a household, and is in many ways very much of an adult and should be considered so.

Sexual materials for young adults, in my opinion, should include more in-depth information on human reproduction, including menstruation, masturbation, sexual intercourse, contraception, and pre-marital sex. These are subjects that many of this age group are encountering and experiencing, and ought to have information about.

As a mother, I would have no objection to my child reading such materials and would expect that many of them could be obtained at my local library. This, of course, would assume that the materials displayed presented human sexuality in a natural, educational manner. My objection would be to presentation by the library of perverted or violent sexual expression which might frighten a child, such as masochism or rape.

Homosexuality, once and, by many people, still considered a perversion, is a subject which might have to be decided by each individual library, but because of its prominence in today's society, it seems only right to me that that segment of society be represented in young adult's literature and be readily accessible to them. After all, some of those young adults will be falling into one of those categories, and they have a right to know about themselves as much as a heterosexual has to know about himself or herself.

Many parents would disagree with me on this point and would argue that reading such literature would encourage homosexuality among young adults, just as reading about pre-marital sex would encourage the child to experience it. However, the Obscenity Commission, appointed in 1968 by President Lyndon Johnson to study, among other things, the effects of obscenity and pornography on the public, particularly minors, found that "such exposure had no measurable impact on their moral character."[3] There was no evidence that exposure to explicit sexual materials played a significant role in causing "delinquent or criminal behavior among youth or adults."[4]

In the light of this study, I am assuming the same would be true of exposure to homosexual literature, i.e., it would not have an adverse effect on young adults and therefore should be available to them in libraries.

Having defined briefly the library's role in a community, the types of sexual materials suitable for a children's library, as well as where the division between children and young adult sections might lie and what kind of materials would be suitable to each, one now faces the crux of the problem of children's rights and their access to information.

If a library has sexual materials available, should they be available to all people regardless of age and/or parental preference, or should they be restricted to certain age groups? When does restriction of materials border on censorship, and when does it violate the Library Bill of Rights? When do I, as a parent, step in and make decisions about what my child is reading?

There are no easy answers to any of these questions, and libraries and city governments have come to blows over the problems more than once, as illustrated in Duane H. Meyers' article on the Oklahoma County Libraries' fight for intellectual freedom in 1975-76.[5]

In this particular case, two young people's books, *Boys and Sex* and *Girls and Sex*, were called into question regarding their propriety in a children's library. The question was first aired in an open letter in the city paper to the executive director of the Oklahoma County Libraries System, and later burgeoned into a full-scale battle between the library and various departments of the county government.

The library's initial stand was to defend its decision to include the two books in its library, stating that there were parents in the community who wished their children to read about sexual matters, and it would be a violation of intellectual freedom for the library to forbid access to that material.

The library stated that "if parents wish to restrict their children's reading, that is their prerogative and the library will respect it."[6] However, those parents could not expect the library to restrict the reading of other people's children.

Later, bowing to political pressure, the library proposed an optional card system, issuing two cards to minors under 15½ years: an unlimited access card and a restricted library card signed by a parent or guardian restricting access to sex education materials. The two controversial books were placed in the restricted access category. Parents who wished their children to have unlimited access to library materials were encouraged to go with their child to the library to get an unrestricted card.

As the Oklahoma controversy continued, it was revealed that the library, in implementing a limited access card policy, was violating the 1969 Library Bill of Rights, which stated that a library should provide service to all people on an equal treatment basis, not differing because of "age, race, religion, national origins, or social or political views."[7]

Finally, the Library Commission sought legal advice on how much and how little it could legally restrict, and after four months of struggle voted to rescind the restrictive policy and return to the previous open access policy.

The two controversial books were classified as "adult," but could be checked out by both adults and children.

The Oklahoma case covers many of the questions on the present debate over children's rights, and library and parental roles with regard to access of children to sexual materials.

In my opinion, reading materials previously selected and available in a library should not be restricted. It is indeed a violation of personal rights to restrict materials, if one has them available. Besides, a child will find what he wants to read through other channels than the public library if he is determined. Personally, I cannot find a defensible reason for a library to carry a book or periodical and to deliberately restrict it to a certain age group for moral reasons.

As far as the parental role is concerned, I feel as a mother that if a parent is concerned about the influence of sexual reading materials on his/her child, the parents should take the responsibility of restricting the child's reading in whatever way works for him/her. If it means accompanying the child each time he/she goes to the library, so be it. The parent's concern should not be thrown on the library's shoulders, nor should the library be forced to make the decisions about what is proper for each child to read. Rather, it should make available a variety of materials which will appeal to diverse tastes. Parents then should be allowed to choose what reading is best for his or her particular child. Many parents will not agree with my views, and that is exactly why it should be an individual matter.

I do feel that it is the responsibility of the library to present responsible materials in the area of sex education. The selection of such materials requires a decision, and ultimately, discrimination, by someone; however, I feel that that someone should not be a librarian making decisions single-handedly.

Rather, a citizen group with the aid of expertise from professional librarians would seem to best serve the needs of a community. Because the tastes of each community vary, citizen input is crucial in selecting materials that will satisfy the community. Professionals in the field would of course provide a guide to literary taste, presentation, and library policy.

I am convinced, after having lived in Europe for the past two years, that Americans are a bit prudish when it comes to the subject of sex. We are still tied to our Puritan backgrounds which shudder at the thought that we have bodies which can derive pleasure from situations other than the singing of hymns in church.

The Europeans are more at home with their sexuality, and their culture has not deteriorated because of it. Perhaps we could learn a lesson from them. With a little more trust in our young people and a little courage to experiment, we might dare to give our children their right to develop their own sense of discrimination. It is only in this way that they can be expected to grow into mature adults.

REFERENCES

1. Z. Horn, "Library Bill of Rights vs. The Racism and Sexism Awareness Resolution," *Library Journal* 102 (June 1, 1977):1254-5.
2. Public Affairs Committee, Inc., Kenneth P. Norwich, *Pornography: the Issues and the Law* Public Affiars Pamphlet No. 477 (New York: 1972).
3. Ibid., p. 18.
4. Ibid., p. 18.
5. Duane H. Meyers, "Boys and Girls and Sex and Libraries: The Chronicle of One Library's Fight for Intellectual Freedom," *Library Journal* 102, no. 4 (Feb. 15, 1977):457-463.
6. Ibid., p. 460.
7. Horn, "Library Bill of Rights," p. 1254-5.

Government Serials

INTO THE HOPPER

(Regularly a quarterly column in *The Serials Librarian,* "Into the Hopper" focuses on, for this special monographic *SL* supplement, the theme of sex in selected government serials.)

SEX THEMES IN FEDERAL SERIALS

Joe Morehead

INTRODUCTION

The content and disposition of matters relating to gender and sexuality are vast. Vast, too, are the interests of the federal government. Ergo, sex and its manifold mysteries permeate the pages of the serial literature produced by the feds. It is with this fractured syllogism that I offer my contribution to this monographic supplement to *The Serials Librarian.* I have the advantage of amateur standing in this enterprise; sex is too important a topic to be left to the experts. My modest aim in these pages is to present a brief survey of subjects that have been the concern of government agencies during the last decade as described in the literature. No attempt shall be made to assay what Blake called "the lineaments of Gratified Desire" nor to compose some monumental Krafft-Ebing version of *Psychopathia Sexualis Federalis.* Those prone to prurience should read no further; the federal treatment of sex is, by and large, as dull as government itself.

SCOPE

A search of the periodical literature during the 1970s shows at least 50 different federal government journals with articles about sex. The diversity of magazines and topics mirrors the various missions of the agencies that spawn them. Supervising vice bureaus and policing massage parlors are concerns voiced in the monthly *FBI Law Enforcement Bulletin.* Sex counseling and sex education training programs are discussed in *Public Health Reports,* a bimonthly of the Health Resources Administration. Aphrodisiacs real or imagined are analyzed in *Psychopharmacology Bulletin,* a quarterly issued by the National Institute of Mental Health. Sex reversal in the bluegill becomes an appropriate topic for discussion in the quarterly *Progressive Fish-Culturist*, a journal of the Fish and Wildlife Service, Department of the Interior. The wanton gyrations of the gypsy moth are the subject of an article in *Agriculture Research*, a monthly of the Department of Agriculture's Science and Education Administration. Margaret Mead writes of sex differences and whether they are innate, learned, or situational in the pages of the *Quarterly Journal of the Library of Congress*. The *Monthly Labor Review* features an article on sex and union membership. And the magazine *Children Today* publishes an article with the piquant title "Do Animals Have Belly Buttons? Sex Education at the Elementary School Level." One could go on at disquisition's length, but I believe this conveys a flavor of the range of subjects prosecuted with lusty vigor by government scribes and guest contributors.

THE SUBJECTS OF SEX

The plentitude of potential subjects and subdivisions is such that if one were to construct a topical hierarchy, its architectonic structure would resemble the mighty United States patent classification scheme or the Great Chain of Being that Pope celebrated in his *Essay on Man*. Thus in the periodical literature we are able to find entries ranging from microcosm to macrocosm, from the "Possibility of Sex Control by Fuged Spermatozoa" *(Journal of Agricultural Research*, May 15, 1925) to "Cherishing and Preserving: Sex Differences and the Life of the World" *(Quarterly Journal of the Library of Congress*, October, 1975). Some links in this sexual chain include Sex and Education, Sex Education, Sex Crimes, Sex in Prisons, Homosexuality, Prostitution, Sex and Disease, Obscenity and Pornography, Children and Sexuality, and Sex and the Military. Within the purview of these headings one finds articles on sexist texts and curricula, the sexual anxieties of medical students, "Guidelines for Marital Sex: An Analysis of Fifteen Popular Marriage Manuals" *(Mental Health Digest*, May, 1970), rape evidence, sexual molestation of children, sexual fantasies of violent and non-violent prison inmates, contraception, coitus interruptus, drugs and sexual behavior, vasectomy and psychosexual damage, married homosexuals, venereal disease and prostitutes, the epidemiology of prostatic cancer, "Let's Put the Smut Merchants Out of Business" *(FBI Law Enforcement Bulletin*, December, 1971), assertiveness training for the military woman *(Air University Review*, January-February, 1978) and gonorrhea for the military man *(Soldiers*, April, 1972).

Sex and Discrimination

Since 1970 well over 200 periodical articles have been listed under the topic "SEX—Discrimination" in the selective *Index to*

U.S. Government Periodicals. Although articles in this area have appeared in journals as disparate as *Business America* and *Army Reserve Magazine,* a few federal magazines stand out in their coverage of matters pertaining to sex and discrimination. Students in this area would do well to peruse the pages of *Civil Rights Digest, Monthly Labor Review, Black News Digest, Women & Work, Civil Service Journal,* and *American Education.* Virtually every aspect of the problem has been treated in article or news release form. Some of the issues in recent years have included the Bakke decision from the feminist perspective, sex inequalities in pension benefits, racism and sexism, pay disparities between men and women, rights of pregnant women, illegal underpayment of black workers, equal pay violations found in stores like Macy's and K Mart, sexual harrassment in job situations, and the like.

The quarterly *Civil Rights Digest* has been issued by the federal Commission on Civil Rights since 1968 and is intended to stimulate interest in every facet of minority problems. The journal is available to depository libraries (CR 1.12; Item 288-A), and non-depository institutions may subscribe to it by writing the issuing agency. The distinguished *Monthly Labor Review* is a depository selection (L 2.6; Item 770) and is available for sale from the Superintendent of Documents. Inexplicably, while most bibliographic sources (including *Price List 36,* the official selection tool for periodicals and subscription services sold by the Superintendent) list it by the above title, the *1979 Serials Supplement* calls it *MLR, Monthly Labor Review.* This little variation is important to remember when you want to call it up by title online with Lockheed's DIALOG (File 66). *MLR* is issued by the Bureau of Labor Statistics of the Department of Labor.

The Labor Department, through its Office of Information, Publications, and Reports, also issues the weekly *Black News Digest* (L 1.20) and the monthly *Women & Work* (L 1.20/8). Unfortunately, these periodicals are neither depository items nor sales items. Both are informative loci of commentary on sex bias topics, and libraries should be able to get on the mailing list to receive them by writing the Office of Information.

Civil Service Journal was recently renamed *Management* but is still the provenance of the Civil Service Commission. A quarterly, it focuses attention on important developments in the Commission's Office of Personnel Management. It is available to depository libraries (C 1.66; Item 290-C) and is available for sale by the Superintendent of Documents.

American Education will, I presume, find a new home with the recently created Department of Education and will be assigned a shining new SuDocs class number. At this writing it is still classed in HE 19.115 and is available to depository libraries as Item 455-B. The monthly has been covering topics from preschool to adult education, research and demonstration projects, major legislation in the field, and lots of information on grants, loans, contracts, and fellowships. Past issues have published articles relevant to the theme of sex and discrimination: changing male roles, counseling as a "superbomb against sexism" (April, 1977), sex bias in the curriculum, and other apposite subjects.

This is but a meager sample. I have found news, articles, and commentary on this significant issue in the *Federal Reserve Bulletin, Military Chaplains' Review, Department of State Newsletter, Air University Review, Extension Review, Social Security Bulletin,* and *Worklife.* The latter, unfortunately, exists no more. Before January, 1976, it was called *Manpower* and classed in L 1.39/9. The Manpower Administration was shamed into changing its sexist title in 1976 when it became the Employment and Training Administration. At that time the magazine re-emerged as *Worklife* and was reclassed in L 37.10. But in 1979 it was discontinued. Earlier issues of *Worklife* and *Manpower* carried useful articles on such subjects as women in the construction and shipbuilding industries, sex bias and vocational education, removing the barriers for women apprentices, and equal protection under the law. It is devoutly to be wished that articles in this area will rapidly diminish, for that will signify a reduction of sex and discriminatory practices.

SEX AND THE SERIAL SET

While the agencies of the executive branch have pursued this perdurable subject, the United States Congress has not remained impotent. The fabled series known variously as the serial number set, sheep set, congressional set, or congressional series has included a number of publications pertaining to matters sexual throughout its long, enigmatic history. In recent years the Serial Set, consisting of House and Senate documents and reports, has seen congressional committee reports pursuant to legislative and investigatory studies on women's rights and International Women's Year (94-1: H.rp. 450), sex discrimination in the appointment of cadets to the Coast Guard Academy (94-2: H.rp. 1109 and 94-2: S.rp. 1186), pregnancy disability (95-2: H.rp. 948 and 95-2: H.rp. 1786), protecting children against sexual exploitation (95-1: S.rp. 601 and 95-1: H.rp. 811), and that surly *bête noire* of government, pornography.

In searching statute or case law on this subject, it is difficult to separate what is "obscene" from what is "pornographic." Indeed, those who assign subject headings to these topics seem not at all sure of the distinction. Perhaps a portmanteau word like "obnography" or "porscenity" (both of which are suitably unpleasant to the ear) should be coined to cover this vexatious aspect of the human condition. During the 91st and 92nd Congresses, the issue produced a flurry of reports. Protecting minors from sexually oriented mail (91-2: H.rp. 908), salacious advertising (91-2: H.rp. 1105 and 91-2: H.rp. 1353), the control of pornography and constitutional rights (91-2: S.rp. 1205), pornographic mail in general (91-2: S.rp. 1217), motion picture projectionists and the District of Columbia obscenity law (91-2: H.rp. 1723), and offensive sexual materials (92-1: H.rp. 273) were some of the publications that made their way into the bound volumes of the Serial Set. The phenomenon some choose to call "smut" has been a lifetime crusade for countless members of the federal establishment, and this absurd expenditure of time has contributed little to the gaiety of nations. Shakespeare's Sonnet 129 is apposite to this endeavor: "The expense of spirit in a waste of shame/Is lust in action..."

SCRATCHING THE SURFACE

If a small sample of the serial literature reveals so explicit an involvement in the encompassing objects of this immense theme, how dispiriting it is to consider that we have scarcely scratched the surface. What salacious Supreme Court rulings lie unnoticed among the thousands of pages of printed reports? What shameless statistical series parade in rows upon rows, gathered by those busy bureaus that record our births, marriages, divorces, offspring? How many census voyeurs have collected and stored data about our beds and belongings, toilets and tragedies, in the huge information banks they own and operate? And what of the aforementioned concupiscent Congress? What intemperate utterances so fill the volumes of debates and proceedings from the *Annals* to the present *Congressional Record* that the Superintendent of Documents felt constrained to classify that serial by the letter "X"?

Given the millions of dollars it costs, it is reasonable to ask why the government gambols so tirelessly on the sexual greensward. Does it merely demonstrate that the *vas deferens* indeed makes a vast difference? But I eschew the simple approach, for I am in quest of the perfect government sex serial, the quintessential annual, the transcendent quarterly, the consummate monthly or weekly. In this brief, documented odyssey it is clear that I have not found it. Perhaps it is buried somewhere in a numbered series like the Smithsonian Contributions to Anthropology. Let us hope that when this ultimate document is discovered, it will be adjudged by the subject specialists of smut neither obnographic nor porscene.

SEXOLOGY: A PERSONAL GUIDE TO THE SERIAL LITERATURE

Barrett W. Elcano
Vern Bullough

Since sex traditionally has been regarded as a taboo topic, periodicals devoted to the subject were almost non-existent until the post World War II period. Usually when references to sex appeared in serials before that time, they did so as part of another topic. Scientific journals, for example, often included references to sex as part of the ongoing effort to explain physiological differences between the sexes, impregnation, hormonal influences, and so forth. Medical and psychiatric journals often included clinical case studies with a strong sexual factor, while legal journals dealt with sexual topics through discussions of such subjects as prostitution. Religious magazines and journals usually put references to sex in terms of general discussions of morality.

Even though these references do exist, the researcher attempting to find them in early periodicals faces great difficulties because often the articles most pertinent to any investigation of sexuality are indexed under some other topic. In our research into serial literature of the 19th and 20th centuries, the key words for finding articles dealing with sexuality in the indexes were marriage and family. Medically oriented articles more often were indexed under the term sex than non-medically oriented ones, but still, many medical articles could only be found by tracing down references to pregnancy, venereal disease, and oddly enough women, a sort of catchall category for marital problems, sexual dysfunction, etc. Legal literature also often included the word "sex" in describing certain kinds of crimes, but it was usually easier to find pertinent articles by looking up such terms as adultery, prostitution, and rape. Religious literature, except that designed for the religious professional, rarely indexed the term sex, but in the professional literature reference terms often appeared under biblical references such as onanism, adultery, and polygamy. Indexers avoided such terms as homosexuality, transvestism, masochism, and similar descriptive terms until the past decade or so. The great variety of serial literature including references to sexuality can be seen by looking at our bibliographies on homosexuality and prostitution,[1] the Goodland bibliography on sex rites,[2] or others.[3]

Sex as a scholarly discipline—sexology, if you will—began in the last years of the 19th century. The first scholarly journal with any kind of publication life was the *Jahrbuch für sexuelle Zwischenstüffen (Yearbook of Sexual Intermediacy)* issued in Berlin from 1899 to 1923 although appearance was not particularly regular after 1914. The editor, publisher, and often the chief writer was Magnus Hirschfeld (1868-1935). Hirschfeld used many pseudonyms for his own writings, and others who wrote for him also used pseudonyms, perhaps to avoid the stigma of writing for a homosexual magazine. Hirschfeld was not a careful editor, and though there are many articles giving insight to ongoing research into human sexuality, particularly homosexuality, there are also many typographical errors, incomplete sentences, missing footnotes, and erroneous citations. The title changes slightly from time to time. There were 23 volumes issued but some were combined. Several libraries have more or less complete runs of the publication, including California State University at Northridge. Hirschfeld joined with Hermann Rohleder and Friedrich S. Krauss to publish the *Zeitschrift für Sexualwissenschaft (Journal of Sexual Science)* in 1908, which lasted until 1930. Most of the volumes can be found at Northridge. It too had an irregular history and a mixed editorial policy. Hirschfeld also published the *Vierteljahrsberichte des wissenschaftlich-humanitären Komitees (Quarterly Reports of the Scientific-Humanistic Committee)* which he had helped to organize in 1897. Occasionally this seems to be combined with the *Jahrbuch* and we have not seen a complete run of this in the course of our researches. Hirschfeld was also involved in founding the International Congress for Sexual Reform, which later became the World League for Sexual Reform. Proceedings of four of the five conferences were published by different English and German publishers. The World League dissolved soon after the 1932 (fifth) Congress because of internal conflict and the growing tension with the outside world.

All the journals with which Hirschfeld was associated tried to list current literature, and often abstracts were included. There was, however, no consistency. The current literature summaries are often based upon the appropriateness of the titles rather than an analysis of content, and comparatively few abstracts were included. The reasons for inclusion or lack of inclusion are not clear. Still, the journals are a valuable guide and often the only one available for the period they cover.

The fact that a journal devoted to research in homosexuality was among the first serious sexological journals is not so unusual as it might appear, since for the most part homosexuality has continued to serve as a major focus of sex research journals. To take some contemporary examples, the *One Institute Quarterly,* which published regularly for about 10 years beginning in 1958, was probably the most scholarly and serious sexological magazine published in the United States during that period. The *Journal of Sex Research,* published by the Society for the Scientific Study of Sex, began publishing in 1965, and the *Archives for Sexual Behavior* in 1971. As the *One Institute Quarterly* gradually disappeared, several new homosexually oriented research journals appeared, including the *Journal of Homosexuality* (1974) and the *Journal of Homosexual Counseling*. About the same time the *Sexual Law Reporter* (1975) began publishing, so that the United States in the late 1970s had about the same range of publications as did Germany 50 and 60 years before. The American journals, like their German ancestors, remain uneven, and though there are occasional literature summaries, and some abstracts, there is as yet no attempt to give comprehensive bibliographies or surveys of ongoing research. Scholarship also remains uneven although there has been a general raising of standards. Probably the most complete abstracting of the periodical literature is the *SIECUS Report* (1972), published bi-monthly by the Sex Information and Education Council of the United States. Less scholarly and less helpful is the journal put out by the AASECT (American Association of Sex Educators, Counselors and Therapists).

In between the start of sexological journals in Germany and the current U.S. crop is a rather ambiguous list of serials. This is due in part to the fact that sexological journals suffered from a basic problem of an ambiguous audience. Though individuals like Hirschfeld, Havelock Ellis, Norman Haire, and Iwan Bloch could perhaps be called sexologists, most of the researchers in the field also wore other hats. They were biologists (such as Alfred Kinsey) or psychiatrists (such as Sigmund Freud) or lawyers (such as Judge Ben Lindsey) or philosophers (such as Bertrand Russell or Rene Guyon). Sexual studies included many different disciplines, and the professional rewards for the most part went to those who published not in sexological journals but in their own professional ones. To be labeled as a sexologist was also a stigma that many found difficult to bear. Moreover, many of those engaged in sex research did so with political goals in mind. The very title of the World League for Sexual Reform emphasizes this reformist goal, and a number of reforms from companionate marriage to contraceptives to the prevention of venereal disease were mixed in with the concept of sex research. In fact, the World League became more or less moribund after the 1932 Congress in Brno, Czechoslovakia, because the two surviving co-presidents differed about what sex reform meant. Norman Haire, the English sexologist, wanted to keep revolutionary politics out of the Congress, while J. H. Leunbach, the other president, believed the sex reform movement would fail unless it embraced the revolutionary workers' movement.

The one thing the disparate groups had in common was a recognition of the need for sex education, but here again there was a problem of an audience. Haire and the group associated with him began publication of *The Journal of Sex Education* in August, 1948, but does such a journal aim at the professional educator or the general public? Such disparate journals as *Sexology* and *Forum* have justified their existence because of their service to sex education. Though these last two occasionally had scholarly articles and have had distinguished sex researchers write for them, it is not clear whether they should be included in a list of serials. On a somewhat higher level is *Medical Aspects of Human Sexuality,* published since 1967 and aimed primarily at the medical community. In the same vein was the shorter lived *Human Sexuality.*

In a sense the journals aimed towards a homosexually oriented audience served the same educational purpose as the above. They, however, had a more consistent readership who were also interested in research findings in order to help them better understand their own homosexuality. Several had rather long periods of publication. *Der Kreis,* for example, began publishing in 1932 in Zurich in German; in 1941 it began to publish articles in French and in 1952 in English as well. The Dutch survivors of the Hirschfeld group began publishing a homosexual magazine, *Vriendschap,* in 1945, and this was soon followed by *Lesbos,* a lesbian oriented publication. There were several homosexual oriented publications in Germany after World War II, probably the first of which was *Die Insel,* which changed its name to *Der Weg. Arcadie* was published in France in 1954. In the United States, the short lived *Vice Versa* was published in 1947 and 1948, and many of the people involved in this eventually ended up publishing *One,* the *Ladder,* and the *Mattachine Review*—the early homosexual magazines. Publishing such magazines meant difficulty with the postal authorities, and it was not until 1958 that *One* (One, Inc. v. Olesen, 241 f, 2nd 772. 9th Gr (1957) and 355 U.S. 271 (1958)) won the right to send its copies through the mails.

Most, if not all, of the homosexually oriented journals were published by homosexuals. This was not the case with publications dealing with prostitution. In fact, most journals dealing with this subject were associated with the abolitionist movement. *Der Abolitionist,* for example, started in 1902 in Dresden, and similar publications were issued in most of the western countries. In the United States most of the journals dealing with prostitution were associated with the American Social Hygiene Association, the Association for Moral and Social Hygiene, or the British Vigilance Association. One of the more helpful in giving extracts and reviews of other periodical literature is the *Bulletin Abolitioniste,* which started in 1879 as *Le Bulletin Continental,* and went through several series, the most recent being in 1949.

Other forms of sexual behavior have not yet attracted quite so much attention as homosexuality and prostitution, although there are serials devoted to such topics as transvestism, bondage, masochism, and swinging (this last the *Journal of Alternate Life Styles* (1978), quarterly, presenting scholarly research on traditional marriage and its alternatives). Most are not particularly scholarly and perhaps are to be compared more with *Playboy, Penthouse,* etc., designed to arouse the interest of their special readers and only incidentally to include more scholarly material. Probably the most rapidly growing field in human sexuality is that of the sex therapist, and a number of journals are beginning to appear in this area. Most of these are oriented to the practicing therapist and this group also is becoming increasingly influential in the revived Sexological Congresses which have been held in Montreal, Rome, and Mexico City. There is also considerable interest in development of gender role among child psychologists, pediatricians, nurses, and teachers to supply enough readership for specialized journals in that area.

What we have done is provide a list of the more recent serials in the sex field, mostly in English. They are divided by subject matter. Many of the serials are in the Institute for Sex Research Library at Indiana University; several can be found at Northridge. Others are in various collections of more specialized literature such as the One Institute Library in Los Angeles or the CHEER group in San Francisco. Coyote has some serials dealing with prostitution, particularly those put out by various local groups. What is needed as sex research assumes more importance is, if not a central depository (which seems unlikely), a union list of sex and sexology research journals accessible by direct user contact or through inter-library loan channels.

SELECTED BIBLIOGRAPHY OF JOURNALS IN SEXOLOGY

SEX RESEARCH

Advances in Sex Research. Hoeber Medical Division, Harper & Row, 49 East 33rd St., NY, NY. Irregular. 1963-

Archives of Sexual Behavior. Plenum Publishing Corp., 227 W. 17th St., NY, NY. Quarterly, 1971-
Very technical articles presenting original research covering all phases of sexuality. Experimental research, psychiatry, and medicine seem emphasized.

Journal of Sex and Marital Therapy. Human Sciences Press, 72 5th Ave., NY, NY. Quarterly. 1974-
Emphasis seems on clinical techniques. Presents "revolutionary" ideas in the practice of sex and marital therapy. Includes book reviews and new product news sections.

Journal of Sex Research. Society for the Scientific Study of Sex, 138 East 94th St., NY, NY. Quarterly. 1965-
Interdisciplinary approach providing broad coverage from health sciences and related behavioral disciplines.

Medical Aspects of Human Sexuality. Hospital Publications, Inc., 18 East 48th St., NY, NY. Monthly. 1967-
Journal is directed toward the physician and provides clinically oriented articles dealing with a broad array of sexual problems. Panel discussions of topics are frequently provided. Includes question and answer section.

SIECUS Report. Sex Information and Education Council of the United States. 1972-

Sex Problems Court Digest. Juridicial Digests Institute, 1860 Broadway, Suite 1401, NY, NY. Monthly. 1970-

Sex Roles; A Journal of Research. Plenum Press, 227 West 17th St., NY, NY. Quarterly. 1975-

Sexology; Educational Facts for Adults. Sexology Corp., 200 Park Ave., NY, NY. Monthly. 1933-
Informational journal directed towards the general reader. Features include "Sex in the News," "Science Notes," and "Sex Scene." Includes questions answered section. Illustrated.

Sexual Behavior. Interpersonal Publications, Inc., 299 Park Ave., NY, NY. Monthly. 1971-
Journal is directed toward the general audience, presenting a wide range of topics. Illustrated.

Sexual Law Reporter. Sexual Law Reporter, 3701 Wilshire Blvd., Suite 700, Los Angeles, CA. Bi-monthly.

Sexuality and Disability. Human Sciences Press, 72 5th Ave., NY, NY. Quarterly. 1978-
Journal is directed toward providing a forum for clinical research and research progress. "Disability" is defined broadly, including physical disabilities, mental illness, and disabling conditions.

Sexuality Today. Atcom Press, 2315 Broadway, NY, NY. Weekly. 1977-

Studies in Sex and Society. Basic Books, Inc., 404 Park Ave., NY, NY. Irregular. 1966-

BIRTH CONTROL

Contraception. Geron-X, Inc., Box 1108, Los Altos, CA. Monthly. 1970–
Essentially, a technical journal for physicians or medical researchers. Articles cover all forms of birth control and family planning.

Fertility and Sterility. Williams & Wilkins, 428 E. Preston St., Baltimore, MD. Monthly. 1949-
Coordinated by the American Society for the Study of Sterility, this publication presents original research and research reports of a technical nature dealing with all aspects of reproduction. Much information on contraceptives is included. Book review section provided.

IPPF Medical Bulletin. International Planned Parenthood Federation, 1820 Lower Regent St., London, SW1, England. Bi-monthly. 1966-
Abstracts of journal articles, reports, and monographs are provided. Listings of new books, films included.

International Planned Parenthood News. International Planned Parenthood Federation, 1820 Lower Regent St., London, SW1, England. Monthly. 1964–
Generally less technical than *IPFF Medical Bulletin*, direction is toward the educated layperson. Coverage of Third World and developing nations seems particularly strong.

Research in Reproduction. International Planned Parenthood Federation. 1820 Lower Regent St., London, SW1, England. Bi-monthly. 1969-
Presentation of original research emphasized. Provides technical notes on advances in reproductive physiology. Includes book reviews and summaries of research.

HOMOSEXUALITY

The Advocate: The Newspaper of American's Homophile Community. Liberation Publications, Inc., 1730 South Amphlet, Suite 225, San Mateo, CA. Bi-weekly. 1967-
Major homophile publication in tabloid form. Features news items and in-depth comment and analysis. Somewhat male oriented and exhibits some West Coast (i.e., California) influence. Includes regular columns on food, body building, advice; provides theatre, film, and book reviews. Interviews with major figures related to the Gay Liberation Movement are frequently provided.

Ain't I A Woman. Box 1169, Iowa City, IA. Irregular.
Essentially a gay woman's paper, orientation seems radical.

Amazon Quarterly. Amazon Press, Box 433, W. Somerville, MA. Quarterly. 1972-
Important lesbian and feminist journal. Editorial policy indicates an emphasis on the woman's movement rather than lesbianism. Well written substantial articles. Includes essays, criticism, and some interviews.

The Body Politic. Pink Triangle Press, 24 Duncan St., P.O. Box 7289, Station A; Toronto, Ontario, Canada. Bi-monthly.
Gay Liberation Movement oriented journal.

Brother. 1721 Grove Street, Berkeley, CA. Semi-monthly. 1971-
Gay Liberation oriented publication, male emphasis.

Chicago Gay Crusader. Box 872, Chicago, IL. Monthly. 1973-

Cowrie. 359 E. 68th St., NY, NY. Irregular.
Lesbian and feminist journal.

David. David Publications, Inc., P.O. Box 5396, Jacksonville, FL. Monthly. 1970-

Detroit Liberator. Box 631-A, Detroit, MI.
Gay Liberation oriented newspaper. Attempts to provide sensitive, "noncamp," unpornographic literature alternative for gays.

Dignity. 755 Boylston, Rm. 514, Boston, MA. Monthly.
The national publication of the gay Catholic community. News and developments within the Roman Catholic Church emphasized.

Drum. Janus Society of America, 1230 Arch St., Philadelphia, PA.

Empty Closet. 713 Monroe, Rochester, NY.
Gay newspaper for the Rochester-Genosee Valley region.

Fag Rag. P.O. Box 331, Kenmore Station, Boston, MA. Quarterly. 1971-
Important tabloid emphasizing news of male gay liberation. Well-written articles, illustrated.

Fifth Freedom. Mattachine Society of the Niagra Frontier, Box 975, Ellicott Station, Buffalo, NY. Monthly.

Focus: A Journal for Gay Women. Boston Daughters of Bilitis, 419 Boylston St., Rm. 323, Boston, MA. Monthly. 1972-
Essentially a mimeographed newsletter providing selected news coverage, letters, advertisements.

The Furies. Box 8843, S.E. Station, Washington, D.C.
A lesbian and feminist publication. Provides analysis of relevant political and social concerns, some fiction, and graphics.

GCN (Gay Community News). 22 Bromfield St., Boston, MA. Weekly.
Gay weekly, in tabloid form with East Coast orientation.

GPU News. Gay Peoples Union, Inc., P.O. Box 92203, Milwaukee, WI. Monthly. 1971-
News reporting publication. Frequently provides short stories and poetry.

Gay. Four Swords, Inc., 116 W. 14th St., NY, NY. Semi-monthly. 1969-
News reporting publication with well-written articles. Fiction is not emphasized. Includes interviews and regularly features book, film, and play reviews.

The Gay Alternative. 232 South St., Philadelphia, PA. Bi-monthly.
"Journal for Gay People."

Gay Book News. 315 Blantyre Ave., Scarborough, Ontario, Canada. Irregular. 1973-
Provides brief book reviews covering items of interest to the full spectrum of gay life. Particularly strong in listing material published by small presses or published privately.

Gay Canadian. Canadian Gay Activists Alliance, Box 284, Station A, Vancouver, British Columbia, Canada. 1971-

The Gay Christian. M(etropolitan) C(ommunity) C(hurch) New York, Box 1757 GPO, NY, NY. 4-6 issues per year.
The journal of the Metropolitan Community Church. Emphasis on news and activities of the MCC. Provides theologically oriented articles.

Gay Dealer. Box 13023, Philadelphia, PA.

Gay Flames. Box 410, Old Chelsea Station, NY, NY.

Gay Liberator. Box 631-A, Detroit, MI. Ceased Spring 1976.
Newspaper of gay activism.

Gay Literature. English Department, California State University, Fresno, Fresno, CA. Quarterly. 1974-
Presents fiction and essays on gay life.

Gay News Gay Guide. Gay News Ltd., 1A Normand Gardens, Greyhound Rd., London, W14 9SB, England. Monthly. 1972-
Gay news reporting publication. Book reviews included.

Gay People and Mental Health. Box 3592 Upper Nicolet Station, Minneapolis, MN. Monthly. 1972-
Brief newsletter (usually 4-6 pages) with notes on books and brief articles. Emphasis is on reporting accounts of and advice for formation of community centers for health services.

Gay Power. 105 Second Ave., NY, NY.

Gay Scene. Gallery Three Enterprizes, P.O. Box 247, Grand Central Station, NY, NY. Monthly. 1970-

Gay Sunshine. P.O. Box 40397, San Francisco, CA. Monthly. 1969-
Important activist, gay liberation oriented newspaper (format has varied in the past). Very well-written in-depth articles concerning related political and social issues. Some emphasis on reporting of local events. Occasional poetry included. Articles seem to emphasize oppression of gays and approaches to that oppression.

Gay Voice. Box 2129, Sacramento, CA.

Gay World. Derek James, 118 Wyndham Road, Bournemouth, Hastings, England.

Homosexual Counseling Journal. 921 Madison Ave., NY, NY. Quarterly.
Clinical articles directed toward professionals dealing with homosexuals.

Hub Newsletter. Box 217, Dorchester Center Station, Dorchester, MA.
Gay Liberation Movement oriented newspaper.

Interchange. 2115 S St., NW, Washington, D.C. Bi-monthly.
The official publication of the National Gay Student Center.

Integrity: Gay Episcopal Forum. Box 891, Oak Park IL.

Journal of Homosexuality. Haworth Press, 149 5th Avenue, NY, NY. Quarterly. 1974-
Important journal providing clinical articles and original research primarily in mental health with frequent material, articles, etc., in other behavioral sciences. Scope covers all aspects of homosexuality and gender identity.

It's Time. National Gay Task Force, 139 Henry St., NY, NY. Monthly.
Newsletter of the National Gay Task Force.

The Ladder. P.O. Box 5025, Washington Station, Reno, NV. 1956- Ceased publication.
Important lesbian journal for the period covered. Provided news, both fiction and non-fiction articles and book reviews.

Lavender Woman. Lavender Woman Collection, P.O. Box 60206, 1723 W. Devon, Chicago, IL. Bi-monthly. 1972-
Lesbian and feminist newspaper, in absence of *The Ladder,* becoming very important national publication. Very well-written articles; earlier emphasis seemed on consciousness raising.

Lesbian Alliance Newsletter. Box 4201, Tower Grove Station, St. Louis, MO. Monthly.

Lesbian Connection. Abitious Amazoru, Box 811, East Lansing, MI. Bi-monthly. 1974-

The Lesbian Feminist. Box 243, Village Station, NY, NY.
Political and arts newsletter.

Lesbian Front. Box 8342, Jackson, MS. Monthly.

Lesbian Lipservice. Gay Women's Advocate Office, 326 Michigan Union, Ann Arbor, MI. Monthly.

Lesbian Reader. Amazon Press, 395 60th St., Oakland, CA. Quarterly. 1975-

Lesbian Tide. 8706 Cadillac Ave., Los Angeles, CA. Monthly. 1971-
Important nationwide lesbian and feminist news reporting publication. Provides national directory of "where it's at." Poetry and graphics included. Some emphasis on the Los Angeles area.

Lesbian Visions. Gay Peoples Union at Stanford, Box 8265, Stanford, CA. Monthly.

Lesbian Voices. Ms Atlas Press, 53 W. San Fernando, San Jose, CA. Quarterly. 1974-

Long Time Coming. Box 161 Station E, Montreal, Quebec, Canada.
Canadian lesbian and feminist newspaper.

Manroot. Box 982, South San Francisco, CA.

Michael's Thing. 200 W. 72d St., NY, NY. Weekly. 1970-

One Institute Quarterly. 2256 Venice Blvd., Los Angeles, CA. Quarterly.
Attempts to present original research; orientation seems toward historical issues.

Out. Foreshadow Publications, P.O. Box E, Old Chelsea Station, NY, NY. Bimonthly. 1974-
Emphasis of journal is directed towards both gay and general audiences. Topics are of general, not always primarily of gay, interest. Poetry and fiction are included. Some emphasis on New York area.

Paragraph: A Quarterly of Gay Fiction. The Antares Foundation, Box 14051, San Francisco, CA. Quarterly.
Full range of gay fiction, art, and satire.

Pointblank Times. Box 14643, Houston, TX.
Lesbian news reporting publication.

RFD. The Northwest Collective, 4525 Lower Wolf Creek Road, Wolf Creek, OR. Quarterly. 1974-
Interesting journal directed toward rural oriented gays. Includes articles, interviews, fiction, poetry, criticism, and art.

Sappho. BCM/Petrel, London, WCIV 6XX, England.
British lesbian journal.

Sisterlife Journal. Feminists for Life, Inc., Box 12726, Tucson, AZ. Quarterly. 1973-
Presents some articles related to lesbian issues.

Sisters. San Francisco Daughters of Bilitis, 1005 Market St., Suite 402, San Francisco, CA.
Presents articles related to the lesbian and feminist communities. Fiction, short stories, and poetry are included. Provides a calendar of events for the San Francisco Bay area.

Trés Femmes. Gay Center for Social Services, 2250 B St., San Diego, CA. 2-4 issues per year.

Vanguard. Vanguard Publications, 203 Clayton St., San Francisco, CA. Quarterly. 1967-
Important journal providing in-depth articles dealing with sexual and social investigations of gay people. Includes book reviews.

Vector. Society for Individual Rights, 83 Sixth St., San Francisco, CA. 1963-
Important journal providing articles covering the full range of gay interests. Article content ranges from current to historical. Particular strength in reporting of news and governmental affairs. Book reviews included.

WICCE. Box 15833, Philadelphia, PA.
Lesbian/feminist newspaper.

Weid: The Sensibility Revue. Olivant Press, P.O. Box 1409, Homestead, FL.
Essentially a review of the literary media.

Yellow Book. Mark Distributors, 712 Greenwich St., NY, NY. Monthly. 1973-
Gay monthly review.

TRANSVESTISM, EFFEMINISM

Double F; A Magazine of Effeminism. Templar Press, Box 98, FDR Station, NY, NY. Irregular. 1972-
Noted for high level of writing. Substantial articles present reports of current issues, prose, and poetry.

Drag. Queens Publications, Box 538, NY, NY. 1970-
Publication is directed toward transvestites and is not concerned with sexual matters *per se*, a "magazine for transvestites without reference to sexual preference." Features news and articles dealing with transvestite interests (e.g., legal repression).

Drag Queen. Neptune Publications, P.O. Box 360, Belmar, NJ. Quarterly. 1973-

Female Impersonator. Neptune Publications, P.O. Box 360, Belmar, NJ. Quarterly. 1972-
Emphasis is graphic, providing little actual reading material. Photographs highlight stage appearances, costume balls, personalities, and show business.

Transvestia. Chevalier Publishing, Box 36091, Los Angeles, CA. Bi-monthly.
Important transvestite publication. While emphasis seems heavily directed toward fiction, articles frequently provide coverage of related issues (legal and health issues most often).

REFERENCES

1. See Vern L. Bullough, Dorr Legg, Barrett W. Elcano, and James Kepner, *An Annotated Bibliography of Homosexuality* (2 volumes, New York: Garland, 1976); Vern L. Bullough, Barret W. Elcano, Bonnie Bullough, and Margaret Deacon, *A Bibliography of Prostitution* (New York: Garland, 1977).
2. Roger Goodland, *A Bibliography of Sex Rites and Customs* (London: George Routledge, 1931).
3. Norman E. Himes, *Guide to Birth Control Literature* (London: Douglas, 1931); John M. Mogey, *Sociology of Marriage and Family Behavior* (The Hague: Mouton, 1971); William Parker, *Homosexuality* (San Francisco: Society for Individual Rights, 1966); *Homosexuality* (Metuchen, NJ: Scarecrow, 1971); Martin Weinberg and A. Bell, *Homosexuality: An Annotated Bibiography* (New York: Harper, 1971); Christoper Tietze, *Bibliography of Fertility Control 1950-1965* (New York: National Committee on Maternal Health, 1965); and for list of others see Flora C. Seruya, Susan Losher, and Albert Ellis, *Sex and Sex Education: A Bibliography* (New York: R. R. Bowker Company, 1972).

A SELECT ANNOTATED BIBLIOGRAPHY OF GAY AND LESBIAN PERIODICALS

Frederick McEnroe

I. INTRODUCTION

Persecuted social minorities create positive identities for themselves by recognizing and transforming their oppression and by giving affirmative interpretation to negative social valuations. Organized minority movements for social liberation strive for public and personal goals: freedom from social discrimination and harassment and the inner dissolution of that form of self-hatred which results from social rejection. Newsletters, magazines, and newspapers play an integral role in the early development of liberation organizations, for such publications help to objectify oppression and transform it into positive identity. They provide a forum for discussion and a means of communication among minority members who are growing into new identities. They also help to educate the encompassing majority about the emergence and nature of the new minority sub-groups. In later phases of a movement, publications diversify in order to fill the needs of an expanding membership.

The modern movement among homosexual people to gain freedom from oppressive laws and prejudice, and to be granted the same rights to life and happiness as are granted to the majority of society's members, began with the writings of the German Karl Heinrich Ulrichs in the 1860s. In 1897, the scientist and student of human sexual behavior Magnus Hirschfeld, founded the Scientific Humanitarian Committee, which is considered to be the first homosexual rights organization. From 1899 to 1923 the Committee issued the quarterly *Jahrbuch für Sexuelle Zwischenstüffen (Yearbook for Intermediate Sexual Types)*. The Committee set itself three goals: to abolish Germany's anti-homosexual law, Paragraph 175; to enlighten society on homosexuality; and finally, to interest homosexual men and women in political action. The activities of the Committee came to an end with the rise of the Nazis in Germany.

In the United States, the first attempt to organize homosexual people was initiated by Henry Gerber, who had become acquainted with the homosexual rights movement in Germany during the First World War. On December 10, 1924, Gerber received from the state of Illinois a charter for his group, the Society for Human Rights. The group managed to publish two issues of *Friendship and Freedom* before Gerber and some other members were arrested by the Chicago police and brought to trial.

Although the case against Gerber was dismissed, it left him broken both spiritually and financially. Nothing more on an organizational level was undertaken for many years. In the interim, especially after the Second World War, homosexual men and women managed to communicate with each other through the personal columns of science fiction club magazines and newsletters and also through those of certain physique magazines.

During the late 1940s, many associations and clubs for homosexual people appeared sporadically in large cities such as New York, Chicago, San Francisco, and Los Angeles. These clubs, formed during the turbulence following the end of the war, began to provide support and identity for homosexual individuals. In June of 1947 there appeared the first lesbian publication in the U.S. It was entitled *Vice Versa* and was produced by a woman named Lisa Ben, who circulated the magazine among her lesbian friends. Because Ben was unable to get others to contribute, *Vice Versa* ceased production in February of 1948.

The 1950s, which saw an increase in the persecution of homosexual people due to the growing conservative trend in American politics, also saw the beginnings of the American homosexual rights movement which has continued to the present day. In April of 1951, the Mattachine Foundation was organized in Los Angeles. Within a year Mattachine discussion groups began to flourish throughout California and in other parts of the nation. In 1952, a group which broke away from the central Mattachine organization began to publish a magazine entitled *One*, whose first issue appeared in June of 1953. The Mattachine reorganized itself as the Mattachine Society and began to publish its own magazine, the *Mattachine Review*, in 1955. Although women had from the beginning played major roles in these organizations, it was the interests of the male members which predominated. In 1955 four lesbian couples in San Francisco founded the Daughters of Bilitis as a support group and organizational center for the needs of lesbians. In October of 1955 they began to publish a magazine called *The Ladder*. Besides their magazines, all three organizations produced newsletters for their membership.

These were the pioneering ventures in homosexual organizing and publishing, but the movement remained very small during the decade. The 1960s saw the beginning of a more activist stance among many homosexual individuals and also an increase in the number of organizations and movement publications. Among such publications were the *Vector* (SF), *The Advocate* (LA), and *Janus Society Newsletter* (Philadelphia). The black civil rights movement and the movement against the Vietnam War provided experience in political organization and activism for many. On June 28, 1969, in New York City, there occurred the riot at the Stonewall Inn which marked the beginning of a new and more radical style in the homosexual rights movement. Younger homosexuals, frustrated by the moderate activism of the older organizations, welcomed radicalism. To symbolize this change the movement was now referred to as Gay Liberation. This new movement spawned a great variety of publications, such as *Gay* in 1968, *Come Out* and *Gay Power* in 1969, *Gay Sunshine* in 1970, *Fag Rag* in 1971, and *Lesbian Tide* in 1972. By 1971 most large American cities and large university campuses had gay liberation groups and gay liberation publications. After 1972 the radicalism of the movement began to wane, while at the same time the movement gained in membership and in political success.

In the early 1970s many lesbians pulled out of gay male dominated organizations and formed either specifically lesbian groups or became involved with heterosexual women in the feminist movement. Lesbians began to address themselves to issues that were of concern to all women, and were in turn supported in their lesbianism by heterosexual feminists. This situation can be seen currently in the many feminist publications in which lesbianism is one among several major concerns rather than being the central focus, as is true in many gay male publications. In the last few years more cooperation has developed between gay men and lesbians both in political action and in the production of publications which are responsive to the needs and concerns of both groups.

II. THE BIBLIOGRAPHY

Homosexual people are as diverse as heterosexual people, and homosexual publications reflect this great diversity. In compiling this bibliography I have attempted to reflect this diversity, while at the same time including publications which are of national and international importance. With one exception *(Lesbian/Lesbienne)*, no publication was annotated which was not examined by the compiler. The bibliography is one of "gay" and "lesbian" periodicals, rather than "homosexual" periodicals, because these are the words typically used to describe the periodicals by those who write and publish them.

The following symbols are used in the bibliography: E, editor; F, frequency; SC, subscription cost; SA, subscription address. All prices quoted are per year unless otherwise noted.

The Advocate

E: Robert I. McQueen
F: Biweekly
SC: 26 issues $15, 52 issues $27

SA: The Advocate
1730 South Amphlett,
Suite 225
San Mateo, CA 94402

One of the oldest and largest gay news magazines, *The Advocate* provides national coverage of events significant to gay men and women in a variety of formats, including news briefs, interviews, cultural and political essays, and reviews of plays, concerts, films, books, the arts, fashion, and sports.

After Dark: The National Magazine of Entertainment

- E: William Como
- F: Monthly
- SC: $18, $34 two years, $48 three years; Foreign and Canada: $21, $40 two years, $57 three years
- SA: After Dark
  Box 950
  Farmingdale, NY 11737

A popular magazine for men, *After Dark* publishes articles on contemporary dance, theater, fashion, music, travel, and personalities.

The BAPHRON

- E: Robert Hindi, MD
- F: Monthly
- SC: $12
- SA: The BAPHRON
  PO Box 14546
  San Francisco, CA 94114

The BAPHRON is the official newsletter of the Bay Area Physicians for Human Rights, an organization of gay San Francisco Bay Area doctors. It publishes essays, news, and reviews of interest to gay and lesbian physicians, medical students, and health workers.

The Blade

- E: Don Michaels
- F: Biweekly
- SC: $8.50 for 24 issues
- SA: The Blade
  2430 Pennsylvania Avenue, N.W.
  Suite 225
  Washington, D.C. 20037

The Blade, "A Publication for the Gay Community" of Baltimore and Washington, D.C., includes national and local news and a calendar of events of interest to both gay men and lesbians.

The Body Politic

- E: The Body Politic Collective
- F: Ten times per year
- SC: Canada: $7.50, $15 first class; International: $10, $20 first class
- SA: The Body Politic
  Box 7289, Station A
  Toronto, Ontario Canada
  M5W 1X9

The *BP* is a major gay magazine from Canada intended to promote "the building of the gay movement and the growth of gay consciousness." It presents, from a radical perspective, news, political and cultural essays and analyses, and reviews of books and cultural events.

Christopher Street

- E: Patrick Merla
- F: Monthly
- SC: $18, $34 two years, $47 three years
- SA: Christopher Street Magazine
  250 West 57th Street, Suite 417
  New York, NY 10019

A literary magazine in a popular format, *Christopher Street* publishes short stories, book excerpts, interviews, essays, poetry, photography, and reviews of books and cultural events.

Chrysalis: A Magazine of Women's Culture

E: Kirsten Grimstad
F: Quarterly
SC: $12, $21 two years, $30 three years

SA: Chrysalis
Department 4152
635 South Westlake Avenue,
Suite 101
Los Angeles, CA 90057

Chrysalis publishes essays on feminist culture, politics, and philosophy, as well as fiction, poetry, and reviews.

Country Women

E: Collective editorship
F: 5 issues per year
SC: $6, $12 institutions, $17.50 foreign

SA: Country Women
Box 51
Albion, CA 95410

A journal for women interested in rural life, each issue is devoted to a particular topic, e.g., humor, spirituality, feminism and relationships, personal power, etc. It publishes poetry, letters, fiction, and practical articles.

Fag Rag

E: Collective editorship
SC: $7

SA: Fag Rag
PO Box 331, Kenmore Station
Boston, MA 02215

Fag Rag is a radical leftist news magazine, published by and intended for feminist identified males. It includes essays, short stories, and poetry.

Gay Academic Newsletter

E: Editorial committee
F: Quarterly
SC: $5

SA: GAU
PO Box 927
Hollywood, CA 90028

Published by the Los Angeles Chapter of the Gay Academic Union, the *Newsletter* includes news items, editorial comments, and reports of ongoing research.

Gay Books Bulletin

E: Wayne Dynes
F: Quarterly
SC: $10, $3 a copy

SA: Gay Books Bulletin
c/o Gay Academic Union, Inc.
P.O. Box 480, Lenox Hill Station
New York, NY 10021

"The *GBB* is dedicated to ... forging an information network providing access to the many channels of homosexual scholarship." This is accomplished through reviews of books by and about homosexuals. Also included are short articles and suggestions for future research.

Gay Community News

E: Richard Burns
F: Weekly
SC: $17.50

SA: GCN Subscriptions
22 Bromfield Street
Boston, MA 02108

GCN presents coverage of national news and events. It also includes reviews and interviews.

Gay Left: A Gay Socialist Journal

- E: Gay Left Collective
- F: Quarterly
- SC: Overseas Airmail: £3 or $6 for 3 issues
- SA: Gay Left
  38 Chalcot Road
  London NW1 England

Gay Left presents in-depth social, political, and cultural analysis of ideas and events from a socialist perspective. It also publishes reviews and lengthy letters. It is mostly of interest to gay men, although it does include some discussion of lesbian issues.

Gay News

- E: Denis Lemon
- F: Fortnightly
- SC: U.S. and Canada, $28 for 13 issues, $54.50 for 26 issues
- SA: Gay News Subscriptions
  1-A Normand Gardens
  Greyhound Road
  London W14 9SB England

Billed as "The World's Largest Circulation Newspaper for Homosexuals," *Gay News* provides a broad coverage of British and European events, and publishes articles, reviews, and an extensive guide to gay and lesbian events in Britain.

Gay Sunshine: A Journal of Gay Liberation

- E: Winston Leyland
- F: Quarterly
- SC: $10
- SA: Gay Sunshine
  PO Box 40397
  San Francisco, CA 94140

Gay Sunshine is known for its lengthy academic analyses of gay male literature and culture and for its in-depth interviews with significant literary figures. It also publishes fiction, poetry, and reviews.

GPU News

- F: Monthly
- SC: $7, two years $12
- SA: GPU News
  PO Box 92203
  Milwaukee, WI 53202

The *GPU News* is a magazine which presents news coverage of national and international events. It also publishes essays, fiction, poetry, and reviews.

Heresies

- E: Collective editorship
- F: Quarterly
- SC: $11, $18 institutions; $2 postage outside U.S. and Canada
- SA: Heresies
  PO Box 766
  Canal Street Station
  New York, NY 10013

Heresies publishes articles and commentary on art and politics from a feminist perspective.

In Unity

- E: Donna J. Wade
- F: Bimonthly
- SC: $8 first class U.S., Canada, Mexico; $8 surface elsewhere; $12 air mail elsewhere
- SA: UFMCC/In Unity
  5300 Santa Monica Blvd.,
  Suite 304
  Los Angeles, CA 90029

In Unity is the magazine of the Universal Fellowship of Metropolitan Community Churches. It publishes notices from various MCC congregations and a selection of articles on theology, fellowship, ministry, and on the relation of gay Christians to the church, politics, sexuality, national events, and the religious life.

Journal of Homosexuality

- E: John P. De Cecco
- F: Quarterly
- SC: $24 individuals, $45 libraries, $42 other institutions
- SA: The Haworth Press
  149 Fifth Avenue
  New York, NY 10010

The *JH* is a scholarly journal devoted to the publication of empirical and archival research on sexual orientation, social sex roles, and human sexuality. It publishes lengthy articles, book reviews, notices of current research in human sexuality, and select annotated bibliographies.

Lesbian/Lesbienne

- E: Collective editorship
- F: Quarterly
- SC: $5
- SA: Lesbian/Lesbienne
  c/o L.O.O.K.
  P.O. Box 2531
  Station B
  Kitchener, Ontario, Canada

This magazine is intended to expand and solidify communication among Canadian lesbians by publishing political articles, news, analysis, and graphics.

The Lesbian Tide

- E: Jeanne Cordova and Sharon McDonald
- F: Six times per year
- SC: $7.50, $9 overseas and Canada, $10 institutions
- SA: Tide Publications
  8706 Cadillac Avenue
  Los Angeles, CA 90034

The Lesbian Tide is a radical feminist news magazine intended to foster open communication by presenting a variety of views from "the lesbian, feminist and gay communities." It publishes news analysis, social commentary, reviews, and advertisements for women's businesses and activities.

The Longest Revolution

- E: Carol Rowell
- F: Biweekly
- SC: $6, $9 outside U.S., $12 institutions
- SA: The Longest Revolution
  CWSS
  908 'F' Street
  San Diego, CA 92101

The Longest Revolution is a newspaper of progressive feminism, which publishes news articles, social and political commentary, and reviews of women's events.

The Montrose Star

- E: Henry McClurg
- F: Weekly
- SC: $21, $29 Canada and Mexico, $39 elsewhere
- SA: The Montrose Star
  PO Box 70282
  Houston, TX 77007

A weekly gay newspaper which circulates throughout the American South and

Southwest, the *Montrose Star* publishes news, short articles, reviews, and local advertisements.

Off Our Backs: A Women's News Journal

    E: Collective editorship
    F: 11 issues per year
    SC: $6, $7 Canada, $13 overseas, $20 businesses and institutions

    SA: Off Our Backs
    1724-20th Street NW
    Washington, D.C. 20009

A lesbian-feminist newspaper that covers national and international events, with a special section on Washington, D.C. It also includes extensive news commentary and analysis.

Out!

    E: Collective editorship
    F: Bimonthly
    SC: $5.00

    SA: Out!
    PO Box 2741
    Station B
    Kitchener, Ontario N2H 6N3
    Canada

Out!, a magazine "dedicated toward eliminating sexual oppression," publishes poetry, short articles, graphics, and advertisements for the Kitchener-Waterloo area of Ontario. It is edited by both women and men.

Outcome: A Magazine of Sexual Politics Produced by Lesbians and Gay Men

    E: Collective editorship
    F: Quarterly
    SC: 2.50 pounds or $5 for 3 issues

    SA: Outcome
    35, West Road
    Lancaster, England

Outcome is a progressive magazine concerned with analysis of English politics and society. It is written by and for both lesbians and gay men.

Plexus

    F: Monthly
    SC: $5 individuals and women-only institutions; $10 other institutions

    SA: Plexus
    2600 Dwight Way, Room 209
    Berkeley, CA 94704

A San Francisco Bay Area women's newspaper presenting a feminist analysis of news and current events. It also includes book and film reviews and a calendar of events.

Quest: A Feminist Quarterly

    E: Dorothy Allison
    F: Quarterly
    SC: $9, $10 Canada and Mexico, $25 institutions

    SA: Quest
    PO Box 8843
    Washington, D.C. 20003

Quest publishes in-depth articles on the theoretical, political, and economic concerns of feminism and the growth of the women's movement. It includes discussions of lesbian issues.

RFD: A Country Journal for Gay Men

E: Collective editorship
F: Quarterly
SC: $6 second class, $8 first class, $7 Canada and abroad, $10 institutions

SA: RFD
Route 1, Box 92E
Efland, NC 29243

RFD publishes articles, poetry, and letters of interest to gay men wishing to explore the values and styles of rural life.

The Sentinel

E: Lydia Shectman
F: Biweekly
SC: $12.50 for 13 issues, $20 for 26 issues

SA: The Sentinel
1042 Howard Street
San Francisco, CA 94103

The Sentinel publishes news, political commentary, reviews of art, literature, and entertainment, and coverage of gay sport events for the San Francisco Bay Area.

SexuaLawReporter

E: Thomas F. Coleman
F: Quarterly
SC: $15 individual, $25 institutional

SA: Sexual Law Reporter
1800 North Highland Avenue,
Suite 106
Los Angeles, CA 90028

The *SexuaLawReporter* is intended to develop a "nationwide communications network" among law reform activists, legal professionals, and legislators concerned with the many facets of sexual law. It presents current information about legislation, court cases, administrative rulings, as well as analytical articles concerning homosexuality, rape, prostitution, abortion, pornography, etc.

Sinister Wisdom

E: Harriet Desmoines and Catherine Nicholson
F: Quarterly
SC: $7.50, $13 two years

SA: Sinister Wisdom
Box 30541
Lincoln, NE 68503

Sinister Wisdom, "A Journal of Words and Pictures for the Lesbian Imagination in all Women," publishes poetry, fiction, photography, articles, and reviews.

Spare Rib: A Women's Liberation Magazine

E: Collective editorship

SC: Airmail to North America, £10.50 or $21

SA: Spare Rib Subscriptions
c/o Linda Phillips
114 George Street
Berkhamsted
Herts Hpf 2EJ, England

A feminist magazine from England presenting articles, fiction, reviews, and advertisements.

III. ADDITIONAL PERIODICALS

Big Mama Rag, 1724 Gaylord Street, Denver, CO 80206. *Feminist monthly.*
Berliner Schwulen Zeitung, c/o Redaktionskollektiv, Postfach 31-15-64, 1000 Berlin 31, Germany. *Radical men's newspaper.*
Campaign, PO Box J41, Brickfield Hill, Sidney NSW 2000, Australia. *Australian gay publication.*
Emanzipation, Postfach 40-05-48, D-8000 München 40, Germany. *German gay liberation magazine.*
Gay Insurgent, PO Box 2337, Philadelphia, PA 19103. *Gay socialist journal.*
The Gay Journal, BBD Publishing, Flat F, 23/24 Great James Street, London, England, WC1N 3ES. *An English gay and lesbian quarterly.*
Gay Life, 205 W. Wacker, Suite 2020, Chicago, IL 60606. *Biweekly newspaper for the Chicago area.*
Gay News German, GNG, D-6242, Kronberg/TS.1, Mainblick 15, Germany. *German news magazine.*
Gay Savoir, ALEPH, 71 rue de Bagnolet, F-75020, Paris, France. *French gay publication.*
High Gear, PO Box 6177, Cleveland, OH 44101. *Gay journal from Ohio.*
Insight, PO Box 5110, Grand Central Station, New York, NY 10017. *Gay Catholic journal.*
New Woman's Times, 1357 Monroe Avenue, Rochester, NY 14618. *Lesbian-feminist newspaper.*
Seattle Gay News, 107 Eastlake Avenue, E., Seattle, WA 98109. *Gay newspaper for Washington state.*

Lists of homosexual periodicals may be found in the following:

Bullough, V. L., Legg, W. D., Elcano, B. W., & Kepner, J. *An Annotated Bibliography of Homosexuality.* New York: Garland Publishing Co., 1976.
Licata, S. J. *Gay Power: A History of the American Gay Movement, 1908-1974.* Unpublished doctoral dissertation, University of Southern California, 1978.
Saunders, D. (Ed.). *Gay Source: A Catalog for Men.* New York: Berkley Publishing Corporation, 1977.

IV. GAY MALE EROTIC PUBLICATIONS

Prior to the freedom of expression gained by the success of gay liberation, the expression of the homosexual imagination was permitted only through the limited medium of erotic and pornographic literature, for the open discussion of homosexuality was allowed in "legitimate" publications only when homosexual characters were depicted as moral villains, social failures, or psychotics. In periodicals the expression of male eroticism took the form of photographs, graphics, and short stories. This tradition of gay male erotica has continued to the present day, and forms both a significant aspect of current gay male culture and of the history of human sexual behavior. No periodicals devoted to lesbian or to women's erotica were discovered by the compiler.

This list represents only a small part of the available material.

Blueboy, 6969 NW 69th St., Miami, FL 33166. *$22.50.*

Drummer, 1730 Divisadero, San Francisco, CA 94115. *Bondage, discipline, and sado-masochistic erotica.*
In Touch, for Men, 1316 North Western Avenue, Hollywood, CA 90023. *$24.*
Mandate: The International Magazine of Entertainment and Eros, 155 Avenue of the Americas, New York, NY 10013. *$26.*
The Manhattan Review of Unnatural Acts, Box 982, Radio City Station, New York, NY 10019. *$6.*
Numbers, 6969 NW 69th St., Miami, FL 33166. *$27.*
Playguy, 155 Avenue of the Americas, New York, NY, **10019.**
Stars, PO Box 28178, Washington, DC. 20005. *$18.*

REFERENCES

Licata, S. J. *Gay Power: A History of the American Gay Movement, 1908-1974.* Unpublished doctoral dissertation, University of Southern California, 1978.

Winter, A. D. *The Gay Press: A History of the Gay Community and its Publications.* Austin, Texas (?): Self-published, typewritten script, 1977 (?).

IF THERE WERE A *SEX INDEX*...

Sanford Berman

There isn't one, of course. Because erotic, gay, and sexologic materials—"dirty," "deviant" books and magazines—have traditionally embarrassed librarians. Even scared them. But the sixties and the sexual revolution have undermined much of that Victorian tradition, producing a real impetus to now actively collect and access that vast, long-neglected, and ever-growing literature of sensuality. So if H. W. Wilson, SIECUS, or Haworth Press *did* produce a *Sex index*—to belatedly complement the *Art index, Business index, Education index,* etc.—it should look something like this:

INDEXED PERIODICALS

Fetish T Fetish Times. B & D Company, P.O.B. 7109, Van Nuys, CA 91409. monthly. $18 p.a.; single issues @ $1.50.
Gay Insurg Gay Insurgent: Journal of Gay Liberation Research, Reviews, and News. "Formerly Midwest Gay Academic Journal." P.O.B. 2337, Philadelphia, PA 19103. 3 nos. yearly. $5 p.a.
Gay Sun Gay Sunshine: a Journal of Gay Liberation. P.O.B. 40397, San Francisco, CA 94140. 8 nos. yearly. $8 p.a.
Hum Dig Human Digest: the Sexual Behavior Journal. Thomaston Publications, 380 Madison Ave., New York, NY 10017. 10 nos. yearly. $10 p.a.; single issues @ $1.25.
J Homo Journal of Homosexuality. Haworth Press, 149 Fifth Ave., New York, NY 10010. quarterly. Libraries: $45 p.a.; institutions: $42; individuals: $24.
Pillow T Pillow Talk: the Monthly Journal of Sexual Fulfillment. Carla Publishing, 208 E. 43d St., New York, NY 10017. $12 p.a.; single issues @ $1.25.
Resp Response: the New Sexuality. Can-Am Media, P.O.B. 909, Fairfield, CT 06430. monthly. $15 p.a.
Screw Screw: the Sex Review. Milky Way Productions, P.O.B. 432, Old Chelsea Station, New York, NY 10011. 10 nos. yearly. $9.95 p.a.; single issues @ $1.50.
Sexol Sexology. Medi-Media Publications, 313 W. 53d St., New York, NY 10019. monthly. $15 p.a.; single issues @ $1.25.
Sex L Reptr Sexual Law Reporter. 1800 Highland Ave. (Suite 106), Los Angeles, CA 90028. quarterly. $30 p.a.
SYOL So's Your Old Lady: a Lesbian/Feminist Journal. 3149 Fremont Ave. S., Minneapolis, MN 55408. bimonthly. $7.50 p.a.; single issues @ $1.25.
Var Variations: For liberated Lovers. Variations Publishing International, 909 Third Ave., New York, NY 10022. bimonthly, beginning Sept. 1979. Special issues @ $2.25.

Sample Entry

RELAXATION
  Altman, Carole
    Too tense for love? Try these relaxation techniques that work!
    Sexol 46-2:39-43 Oct 79

        An article on the subject of relaxation, written by Carole Altman and titled "Too tense for love? Try these relaxation techniques that work!," appears in *Sexology*, volume 46, number 2 (October 1979), on pages 39-43.

Abbott, Keith
  Rhino Ritz.
    Review (Michael Perkins): Screw 548:21 Sep 3, 79

Abbott, Steve
  Wrecked hearts; raw poetry.
    Review (R. Daniel Evans): Gay Sun 40/41:35 Sum/Fall 79

ACTORS, FILM. *See* EROTIC FILM ACTORS.

ADOLESCENT SEXUALITY. *See* TEENAGERS' SEXUALITY.

ADULT BOOKSHOPS. *See* SEX SHOPS.

ADULT-CHILD RELATIONS. *See* BOY LOVE; CHILD MOLESTING; FATHER-DAUGHTER INCEST; MOTHER-SON INCEST; PEDOPHILIA.

ADVERTISEMENTS, PERSONAL. *See* PERSONAL ADVERTISEMENTS.

AFTERPLAY—PERSONAL ACCOUNTS
  Cordially yours [letter]. Sexol 46-2:63 Oct 79

AIDS, SEX. *See* SEX AIDS.

AIRPLANE SEX—PERSONAL ACCOUNTS
  Joy stick [letter]. Var spec 5:94-5 Mid-Spr 79

ALCOHOLIC LESBIANS. *See* LESBIAN ALCOHOLICS.

ALTERNATIVE PRESS DISTRIBUTORS
  Tsang, Daniel
    Radical distribution. Gay Insurg 4/5:12-13 Spr 79

Altman, Carole
  Too tense for love? Try these relaxation techniques that work!
  Sexol 46-2:39-43 Oct 79

AMPUTEES
  The amateur surgeon: "permanent public bondage" the roots of amputee love. Fetish T 64:16-17
  One-legged [letter]. Hum Dig 3-1:57-9 Jan 79

ANAL SEX
  Anal fear [letter]. Hum Dig 3-1:89-90 Jan 79

ANAL SEX—PERSONAL ACCOUNTS
  Anal love [letter]. Var spec 5:161-2 Mid-Spr 79
  Delectable delirium [letter]. Var spec 5:162 Mid-Spr 79
  Lawrence, Adele
    A virgin doesn't have to say no. Var spec 5:105-11 Mid-Spr 79

ANALINGUS
  Miller, Kate
    Analingus: Something special for your lover. Hum Dig 3-1:32-4 Jan 79

Andrews, Martha
  Brief resolution [poem]. SYOL 21: 14 Oct 79

ANDROGYNY
  Bernard, Larry Craig
    Androgyny scores of matched homosexual and heterosexual males. By Larry Craig Bernard and David J. Epstein. J Homo 4-2:169-78 Win 78

ANIMAL LOVE. See BESTIALITY.

ANTI-GAY PREJUDICE. See HOMOPHOBIA.

Antler
  Poems. Gay Sun 40/41:36 Sum/Fall 79

ARCHIVES, GAY. See GAY ARCHIVES.

ARCHIVES, LESBIAN-FEMINIST. See LESBIAN-FEMINIST ARCHIVES.

ARMPIT HAIR
  Passion pit [letter]. Sexol 46-2:62-3 Oct 79

Arrizabalaga y Prado, Leonardo de
  Song without words [poem]. Gay Sun 40/41:35 Sum/Fall 79

"ASS-FUCKING." See ANAL SEX.

Austen, Roger
  Playing the game: the homosexual novel in America. 1977.
    Review (Byrne R. S. Fone): J Homo 4-2: 195-200 Win 78

AUTOEROTICISM. See MASTURBATION.

B/D. See BONDAGE AND DISCIPLINE.

BACCHANALIA
  Brock, Paul
    Pompeii: the first city of sexual freedom. A look at the true meaning of Bacchanalia. Sexol 46-2:19-22 Oct 79

BALDNESS FETISH
  Bald is bawdy! [letter]. Fetish T 64:10

BALLS, BEN-WA. See BEN-WA BALLS.

Bataille, Georges
  Blue of noon.
    Review (Michael Perkins): Screw 548:21 Sep 3, 79

BEACHES, NUDE. See NUDE BEACHES.

Beame, Jeffery
  Tonight desire has a man in it [poem]. Gay Sun 40/41:37 Sum/Fall 79

Beckley, Tim
  Sex at the roller disco. Pillo T 3-6: 62-6 Sep 79

BEN-WA BALLS
  Delectable delirium [letter]. Var spec 5:162 Mid-Spr 79
  Phillips, Kate
    Ben Wa balls: a woman's secret delight. Var spec 5:96-9 Mid-Spr 79

Bentley, Caryl B.
  A both/and song for the crones: dedicated to Mary Daly [poem]. SYOL 21:5 Oct 78

Berman, Sanford
  Gay access: new approaches in cataloging. Gay Insurg 4/5:14-15 Spr 79

Bernard, Larry Craig
  Androgyny scores of matched homosexual and heterosexual males. By Larry Craig Bernard and David J. Epstein. J Homo 4-2: 169-78 Win 78

BESTIALITY
Witomsky, T. R.
Oh, you big brute, you. Pillow T 3-6:12-15 Sep 79

BESTIALITY—PERSONAL ACCOUNTS
Doggie-do [letter]. Resp 6-9:26-6 Oct 79

BIG BROTHERS, INC.
Sexual preference of Big Brothers may be subject to scrutiny. Sex L Reptr 4-4:74 Oct/Dec 78

BIRTH CONTROL—LAWS AND REGULATIONS
Distribution of contraceptives to minors may violate parents' Constitutional rights. Sex L Reprt 4-4:63 Oct/Dec 78

BISEXUALS
See also Swinging
Threesomes

BISEXUALS—PERSONAL ACCOUNTS
Bisexual husband [letter]. Var spec 5:28-8 Mid-Spr 79
Bisexual swingers [letter]. Var spec 5:52-4 Mid-Spr 79
Bisexual threesome [letter]. Var spec 5:29 Mid-Spr 79
Bisexual wife [letter]. Var spec 5:28 Mid-Spr 79
Fellatio fan [letter]. Var spec 5:29-30 Mid-Spr 79
Friends and lovers [letter]. Var spec 5:83-4 Mid-Spr 79
Kempler, Jana
A couple takes a chance. Var spec 5:70-81 Mid-Spr 79
Unforgettable melody [letter]. Var spec 5:84-5 Mid-Spr 79
A yacht to learn [letter]. Var spec 5:82 Mid-Spr 79

Blakeston, Oswell
The graveyard [poem]. Gay Sun 40/41:37 Sum/Fall 79

Bliss, K. D.
Beating the short time Charlie blues. Resp 6-9:27-31 Oct 79

"BLOW JOBS." See FELLATIO.

BONDAGE AND DISCIPLINE
See also Eunuchs
Sadomasochism
The amateur surgeon: "permanent public bondage" the roots of amputee love. Fetish T 64:16-17
Bisexual wife [letter]. Var spec 5:28 Mid-Spr 79
Prolong the agony! [letter]. Fetish T 64:9
Stryker, Rod
On the rack. Fetish T 64:12-13
Von Eckmann, Erika
A eunuch in every garage [letter]. Fetish T 64:9-10

BONDAGE AND DISCIPLINE FANTASIES
The captured maiden [letter]. Var spec 5:42-3 Mid-Spr 79
A rebellious wench [letter]. Var spec 5:41-2 Mid-Spr 79

BONDAGE AND DISCIPLINE IN TELEVISION
Park, R. L.
Bondage on the boob tube. Fetish T 64:11

BONDAGE AND DISCIPLINE—PERSONAL ACCOUNTS
Christie's book: a life in bondage. Hum Dig 3-1:35-6 Jan 79
Friendly, Suzanne
I can be very friendly. Pillow T 3-6:8-10 Sep 79
White slave [letter]. Hum Dig 3-1:63-6 Jan 79

Bonner, T. Pete
Playing the personals. Resp 6-9:32-8 Oct 79

BOOK REVIEWS
•Abbott, Keith
Rhino Ritz.
Review (Michael Perkins): Screw 548:21 Sep 3, 79

•Abbott, Steve
Wrecked hearts; raw poetry.
Review (R. Daniel Evans): Gay Sun 40/41:35 Sum/Fall 79
•Austen, Roger
Playing the game: the homosexual novel in America, 1977.
Review (Byrne R. S. Fone): J Homo 4-2:195-200 Win 78
•Bataille, Georges
Blue of noon.
Review (Michael Perkins): Screw 548:21 Sep 3, 79
•Bullough, Vern L.
An annotated bibliography of homosexuality. 1976.
Review (A. P. M. Coxon): Gay Insurg 4/5:49 Spr 79
Review (William Parker): J Homo 4-2:185-92 Win 78
•Burroughs, William S.
Blade runner: a movie.
Review (Michael Perkins): Screw 548:21 Sep 3, 79
•Christian, Paula
Edge of twilight. 1959.
This side of love. 1963.
Reviews (S.C.): SYOL 21:22 Oct 78
•Crew, Louie
The Gay academic. 1978.
Review (Jim Monahan): Gay Insurg 4/5:43-7 Spr 79
•Curzon, Daniel
Among the carnivores. 1979.
Review (Scott Jones): Gay Sun 40/41:32 Sum/Fall 79
•Dover, Kenneth J.
Greek homosexuality. 1978.
Review (Arthur William Rudolph): Gay Sun 40/41:33-4 Sum/Fall 79
•Evans, Arthur.
Witchcraft and the Gay counterculture. 1978.
Review (Will Inman): Gay Sun 40/41:31-2 Sum/Fall 79
•Fisher, Pete
Special teachers/special boys. 1979.
Review (Scott Jones): Gay Sun 40/41:32 Sum/Fall 79
•Friedman, Leslie
Sex role stereotyping in the mass media: an annotated bibliography. 1974.
Review (Scott D. McDonald): J Homo 4-2:192-4 Win 78
•Gay Theory Work Group of the Movement for a New Society
Gay oppression and liberation, or Homophobia: its causes and cure. 1977.
Review (Marc Killinger): Gay Insurg 4/5:37-42 Spr 79
•Gibson, E. Lawrence
Get off my ship. 1978.
Review (Daniel Tsang): Gay Insurg 4/5:47 Spr 79
•Ginsberg, Allen
To Eberhart from Ginsberg; a letter about HOWL. 1976.
Allen Ginsberg journals; early Fifties early Sixties. Edited by Gordon Ball. 1977.
Mind breaths; poems 1972-1977. 1977.
As ever; the collected correspondence of Allen Ginsberg and Neal Cassady. Edited by Barry Gifford. 1977.
Reviews (David Chura): Gay Sun 40/41:15-16 Sum/Fall 79
•Hamilton, Wallace
David at Olivet, 1979.
Review (Scott Jones): Gay Sun 40/41:32 Sum/Fall 79
•Kelly, Dennis
Chicken; boy love poems. 1979.
Review (Charley Shively): Gay Sun 40/41:9 Sum/Fall 79
•Kirmani, Awhaduddin
Heart's witness; the Sufi quatrains of Awhaduddin Kirmani. Translated by Bernd Manuel Weischer & Peter Lamborn Wilson. 1978.
Review (Winston Leyland): Gay Sun 40/41:33 Sum/Fall 79
•Kramer, Larry
Faggots. 1978.
Review (Larry Puchall): Gay Sun 40/41:34 Summer/Fall 79
•Leyland, Winston
Now the volcano: an anthology of Latin American Gay literature. 1979.

Review (E.A. Lacey): Gay Sun 40/41:26-31 Sum/Fall 79
• Mariah, Paul
This light will spread: selected poems 1960-1975. 1978.
Review (Steve Abbott): Gay Sun 40/41:34 Sum/Fall 79
• Morin, Stephen F.
"The Gay movement and the rights of children." J of Social Issues. 1978.
Review (Daniel Tsang): Gay Insurg 4/5:48 Spr 79
• Orlovsky, Peter
Clean asshole poems & smiling vegetable songs. 1978.
Review (Charles Shively): Gay Sun 40/41:15 Sum/Fall 79
• Parker, William
Homosexuality bibliography: Supplement, 1970-1975. 1977.
Review (Daniel Tsang): Gay Insurg 4/5:49 Spr 79
• Rimbaud, Arthur
Rimbaud/Verlaine: a lover's cock. 1979.
Review (Arthur William Rudolph): Gay Sun 40/41:38 Sum/Fall 79
• Ronan, Richard
Flowers; poems. 1978.
Review (E. A. Lacey): Gay Sun 40/41:32 Sum/Fall 79
• Satin, Mark
New Age politics, healing self and society; the emerging new alternative to Marxism and Liberalism. 1978.
Review (Mitch Walker): Gay Sun 40/41:35 Sum/Fall 79
• Tiktin, Carl
Ron. 1979.
Review (Scott Jones): Gay Sun 40/41:32 Sum/Fall 79
• Watmough, David
No more into the garden. 1978.
Review (Scott Jones): Gay Sun 40/41:32 Sum/Fall 79
• White, Edmund
Nocturnes for the King of Naples. 1978.
Review (Scott Jones): Gay Sun 40/41:32 Sum/Fall 79

Borchette, Suzanne

A night in Central Park. Var spec 5:86-91 Mid-Spr 79

Boston/Boise Committee
Suggestions for media on handling alleged sex "crimes" involving Gay men. Gay Insurg 4/5:56-9 Spr 79

BOY LOVE
Nichols, D. W.
A boy lover's perspective; D. W. Nichols interviewed by Daniel Tsang, Part II. Gay Insurg 4/5:25-36 Spr 79

BOY LOVE—PERSONAL ACCOUNTS
Pedophiliac [letter]. Hum Dig 3-1:92 Jan 79

BOY LOVE—POETRY—REVIEWS
• Kelly, Dennis
Chicken; boy love poems. 1979.
Review (Charles Shively): Gay Sun 40/41:9 Sum/Fall 79
• Kirmani, Awhaduddin
Heart's witness; the Sufi quatrains of Awhaduddin Kirmani. Translated by Bernd Manuel Weischer & Peter Lamborn Wilson. 1978.
Review (Winston Leyland): Gay Sun 40/41:33 Sum/Fall 79

BOY PROSTITUTES. See CHILD PROSTITUTES; MALE PROSTITUTES.

BREAST FEEDING
Breast-feeding [letter]. Hum Dig 3-1:91-2 Jan 79

BREAST PLAY
Hodges, Parker
That misunderstood erogenous zone; the nipple—a powerful source of erotic pleasure in both men and women—is largely unexplored. Sexol 46-2:30-4 Oct 79

BREAST SIZE
A big bust [letter]. Sexol 46-2:61-2 Oct 79

BREASTS
Doolittle, Arch
A global view of breasts. Resp 6-9:40-5 Oct 79

Brock, Paul
Pompeii: the first city of sexual freedom. A look at the true meaning of Bacchanalia. Sexol 46-2:19-22 Oct 79

BROTHER-SISTER INCEST—PERSONAL ACCOUNTS
Incestuous seeker [letter]. Hum Dig 3-1:81-3 Jan 79

Bullough, Vern L.
An annotated bibliography of homosexuality. 1976.
Review (William Parker): J Homo 4-2:185-92 Win 78
Review (A. P. M. Coxon): Gay Insurg 4/5:49 Spr 79

Burleson, Tom
Sensual mind control [story]. Var spec 5:32-7 Mid-Spr 79

BURLESQUE SHOWS
Wife depressed over sex shows [letter]. Sexol 46-2:73-5 Oct 79

Burroughs, William S.
Blade runner: a movie.
Review (Michael Perkins): Screw 548:21 Sep 3, 79

CAB SEX. *See* TAXICAB SEX.

Califia, Pat
Pleasure/pain and power—a Lesbian's view. Var spec 5:56-65 Mid-Spr 79

CALL GIRLS. *See* FEMALE PROSTITUTES.

CAREER WOMEN
Deni, Laura
Why nice girls finish last. Pillow T 3-6:16-21 + Sep 79

CARRIAGE SEX—PERSONAL ACCOUNTS
Borchette, Suzanne
A night in Central Park. Var spec 5:86-91 Mid-Spr 79

CARRIER PIGEON (FIRM)
Tsang, Daniel
Radical distribution. Gay Insurg 4/5:12-13 Spr 79

CARTOONS
Jordon, Flash
Dildonuts [cartoon]. Screw 548: 24-5 Sep 3, 79
Moon, Little
Doping it out [illustrated limericks]. Screw 548:9-11 Sep 3, 79

CASTRATION
Von Eckmann, Erika
A eunuch in every garage [letter]. Fetish T 64:9-10

CATALOGING OF GAY MATERIALS
Berman, Sanford
Gay access: new approaches in cataloging Gay Insurg 4/5:14-15 Spr 79

Catherine, Eleanor
It happened on a train. Var spec 5:116-20 Mid-Spr 79

Chadwick, Jerah
Making it new [poem]. Gay Sun 40/41:35 Sum/Fall 79

CHILD-ADULT RELATIONS. *See* BOY LOVE; CHILD MOLESTING; FATHER-DAUGHTER INCEST; MOTHER-SON INCEST; PEDOPHILIA.

CHILD MOLESTING—LAWS AND REGULATIONS
Age mistake is defense to child molestation. Sex L Reptr 4-4:69 Oct/Dec 78

CHILD "PORNOGRAPHY"
Nichols, D. W.
A boy lover's perspective; D. W. Nichols interviewed by Daniel Tsang, Part II. Gay Insurg 4/5: 25-36 Spr 79
Youth Liberation

Children and sex: a Youth Liberation view. Gay Insurg 4/5:22-4 Spr 79

CHILD PROSTITUTES
See also Boy love
Urban tragedy [letter]. Sexol 46-2:61 Oct 79

Youth Liberation
Children and sex: a Youth Liberation view. Gay Insurg 4/5:22-4 Spr 79

CHILDREN, GAY. See GAY CHILDREN.

CHILDREN'S RIGHTS
Distribution of contraceptives to minors may violate parents' Constitutional rights. Sex L Rptr 4-4:63 Oct/Dec 78
Youth Liberation
Children and sex: a Youth Liberation view. Gay Insurg 4/5:22-4 Spr 79

CHILDREN'S SEXUALITY
See also Boy love
Child "pornography"
Child prostitutes
Gay children
Incest
Pedophilia
Youth Liberation
Children and sex: a Youth Liberation view. Gay Insurg 4/5:22-4 Spr 79

CHILDREN'S SEXUALITY—PERSONAL ACCOUNTS
Chalking it up [letter]. Var spec 5:159-60 Mid-Spr 79
Childhood erotic memories [letter]. Var spec 5:150-6 Mid-Spr 79

Christian, Paula
Edge of twilight. 1959.
This side of love. 1963.
Reviews (S.C.): SYOL 21:22 Oct 78

CHROMOTHERAPY
Jackson, Martin A.
How color affects your life and love. Pillow T 3-6:77-81+ Sep 79

CIRCUMCISION—PERSONAL ACCOUNTS
A satisfied reader [letter]. Sexol 46-2:63 Oct 79

CLUBS, SWINGERS'. See SWINGERS' CLUBS.

COITAL POSITIONS
See also Heterosexual intercourse
Homosexual intercourse
Karlen, Arno
Who's on top? The sexual conflict people don't talk about. Sexol 46-2:24-9 Oct 79

COITUS. See HETEROSEXUAL INTERCOURSE; HOMOSEXUAL INTERCOURSE.

Colebrook, Val
Inside out [poem]. SYOL 21:24 Oct 78
Strange songs (dreams) [poem]. SYOL 21:15 Oct 78

COLOR PSYCHOLOGY
Jackson, Martin A.
How color affects your life and love. Pillow T 3-6:77-81+ Sep 79

CONSUMER GUIDES. See BOOK REVIEWS; ENCYCLOPEDIA EVALUATION; EROTIC FILMS—REVIEWS; GAY FILMS—REVIEWS; SEX AIDS—EVALUATION.

Cooperstock, David
The joys of sex without an erection. Var spec 5:12-17 Mid-Spr 79

COPROPHILIA
Witomski, T. R.
Beyond the last taboo. Var spec 5:136-40 Mid-Spr 79

Corinne, Tee
  The lady who loved horses [graphic]. SYOL 21:24 Oct 78

COUNSELING, SEX. See SEX COUNSELING AND THERAPY.

Cozad, William
  Cruisin' the Bay Area. Resp 6-9:52-6 Oct 79

Crew, Louie
  The Gay academic. 1978.
    Review (Jim Monahan): Gay Insurg 4/5:43-7 Spr 79

Crown, Sandra
  Female sexual fulfillment: what it really means. Hum Dig 3-1:39-45 Jan 79

Cruikshank, Peg
  Notes on two films: Julia and Word is out. SYOL 21:11 Oct 78

CUNNILINGUS
  Small, Larry
    Hot licks: a guide to cunnilingus. Resp 6-9:46-50 Oct 79

CUNNILINGUS—PERSONAL ACCOUNTS
  A fellow traveler [letter]. Sexol 46-2:55 Oct 79
  Home help [letter]. Var spec 5:100-1 Mid-Spr 79
  Lawrence, Adele
    A virgin doesn't have to say no. Var spec 5:105-11 Mid-Spr 79
  Little Miss Muffet [letter]. Var spec 5:157-8 Mid-Spr 79

"CUNT SHAVING." See PUBIS SHAVING.

"CUNT SUCKING." See CUNNILINGUS.

Curzon, Daniel
  Among the carnivores. 1979.
    Review (Scott Jones): Gay Sun 40/41:32 Sum/Fall 79

Dailey, Jan
  Women and orgasm: how to achieve it no matter what. Sexol 46-2:10-18 Oct 79

DATING
  Smith, Belle
    Sexual myths. Hum Dig 3-1:46-9 Jan 79

Dean, Charles
  Reflections of a rapist. Sexol 46-2:44-5 Oct 79

Deni, Laura
  Why nice girls finish last. Pillow T 3-6:16-21+ Sep 79

Diamond, Deborah L.
  Alcohol abuse among Lesbians: a descriptive study. J Homo 4-2:123-42 Win 78

DIAPER FETISH—PERSONAL ACCOUNTS
  Diaper lover [letter]. Var spec 5:160-1 Mid-Spr 79

DILDOS
  Double dong [letter]. Var spec 5:101-2 Mid-Spr 79
  Little Miss Muffet [letter]. Var spec 5:157-8 Mid-Spr 79

DILDOS—CARTOONS
  Jordon, Flash
    Dildonuts [cartoon]. Screw 548:24-5 Sep 3, 79

DISCIPLINE. See BONDAGE AND DISCIPLINE.

DISCO SKATING
  Beckley, Tim
    Sex at the roller disco. Pillow T 3-6:62-6 Sep 79

DISCRIMINATION AGAINST GAYS. See HOMOPHOBIA.

DOLLS, SEX. See SEX DOLLS.

DOMINATION. *See* BONDAGE AND DISCIPLINE.

Doolittle, Arch
A global view of breasts. Resp 6-9:40-5 Oct 79

Dover, Kenneth J.
Greek homosexuality. 1978. Review (Arthur William Rudolph): Gay Sun 40/41:33-4 Sum/Fall 79

DRUGS AND SEX
Moon, Little
Doping it out [illustrated limericks]. Screw 548:9-11 Sep 3, 79

Duncan, Robert
Interview. Gay Sun 40/41:1-8 Sum/Fall 79

ELDERLY PEOPLE'S SEXUALITY. *See* SENIORS' SEXUALITY.

ELECTRIC HAIRDRYERS. *See* HAIRDRYERS.

ELEVATOR SEX—PERSONAL ACCOUNTS
Elevated sex [letter]. Var spec 5:92 Mid-Spr 79

ENCYCLOPEDIA EVALUATION
SantaVicca, Edmund F.
Evaluating encyclopedias: a framework summary. Gay Insurg 4/5:15-17 Spr 79

ENEMA FILMS—CATALOGS
Film fare [advertisement]. Fetish T 64:15

ENGLISH CULTURE. *See* BONDAGE AND DISCIPLINE.

ERECTIONS
See also Impotence
Penis size
Cooperstock, David
The joys of sex without an erection. Var spec 5:12-17 Mid-Spr 79

EROTIC BOOKS
See also Erotic fiction
Stryker, Rod
On the rack. Fetish T 64:12-13

EROTIC FICTION—REVIEWS
•Bataille, Georges.
Blue of noon.
Review (Michael Perkins): Screw 548:21 Sep 3, 79
•Burroughs, William S.
Blade runner: a movie.
Review (Michael Perkins): Screw 548:21 Sep 3, 79

EROTIC FILM ACTORS—INTERVIEWS
Hoffman, Lisa
A bisexual wedding; interview and photos. Porn film star Marc Stevens married transsexual model Jill Monro. Var spec 5:18-27 Mid-Spr 79

EROTIC FILMS
Gersten, Leon
"The fantasy game." Pillow T 3-6:91-3 Sep 79
Helping hand [letter]. Hum Dig 3-1:73-4 Jan 79

EROTIC FILMS—CATALOGS
Your favorite XXX full-length movies are now on video tapes! [advertisement]. Screw 548:8 Sep 3, 79

EROTIC FILMS—REVIEWS
Neuhaus, Manny
Kennel ration raunch [review of Fulfilling young cups]. Screw 548:23 Sep 3, 79
Perkowski, Donald
A flesh start: video vice. Screw 548:17 Sep 3, 79

EROTIC PERIODICALS—REVIEWS
Easy to be hard-core; Screw re-

views issue no. 4 of the graphic glossy gash mag Puritan. Screw 548:4-7 Sep 3, 79

ETHICS, SEXUAL. See SEXUAL ETHICS.

EUNUCHS
Von Eckmann, Erika
A eunuch in every garage [letter]. Fetish T 64:9-10

Evans, Arthur
Witchcraft and the Gay counterculture. 1978.
Review (Will Inman): Gay Sun 40/41:31-2 Sum/Fall 79

EXERCISE
Altman, Carole
Too tense for love? Try these relaxation techniques that work! Sexol 46-2:39-43 Oct 79

EXERCISE FOR WOMEN
Large vagina [letter]. Hum Dig 3-1:80-1 Jan 79

EXHIBITIONISM
See also Nude beaches

EXHIBITIONISM—PERSONAL ACCOUNTS
The balcony [letter]. Var spec 5:121-2 Mid-Spr 79
Catherine, Eleanor
It happened on a train. Var spec 5:116-20 Mid-Spr 79
Chasing the commuter blues [letter]. Var spec 5:123-4 Mid-Spr 79

EXTRAMARITAL RELATIONS
See also Brother-sister incest
Homosexuality
Mate-swapping
Mother-son incest
Swinging

EXTRAMARITAL RELATIONS—PERSONAL ACCOUNTS
Fighting VD [letter]. Hum Dig 3-1:97 Jan 79

A glorious discovery [letter]. Sexol 46-2:57-9 Oct 79
Sexual freedom [letter]. Hum Dig 3-1:67-8 Jan 79
Uptight hubby [letter]. Hum Dig 3-1:86-7 Jan 79

FANTASIES
See also Bondage and discipline fantasies
Rape fantasies
Sadomasochist fantasies
Gersten, Leon
"The fantasy game." Pillow T 3-6:91-3 Sep 79

FANTASIES—FICTION
Burleson, Tom
Sensual mind control [story]. Var spec 5:32-7 Mid-Spr 79

FANTASIES—PERSONAL ACCOUNTS
Califia, Pat
Pleasure/pain and power—a Lesbian's view. Var spec 5:56-65 Mid-Spr 79
The captured squaw [letter]. Var spec 5:39-40 Mid-Spr 79
Cold comfort [letter]. Var spec 5:103 Mid-Spr 79
Female fantasy [letter]. Var spec 5:40 Mid-Spr 79
Rape fantasy [letter]. Var spec 5:38 Mid-Spr 79
Scenes [letter]. Var spec 5:40-1 Mid-Spr 79

FATHER-DAUGHTER INCEST—PERSONAL ACCOUNTS
Father knows best [letter]. Resp 6-9:19-23 Oct 79

FATHERS, GAY. See GAY FATHERS.

FELLATIO—PERSONAL ACCOUNTS
Bedpost fun [letter]. Var spec 5:102-3 Mid-Spr 79
A daring debut [letter]. Var spec 5:114-15 Mid-Spr 79

Fellatio fan [letter]. Var spec 5:29-30 Mid-Spr 79
Furtive fellatio [letter]. Var spec 5:92-3 Mid-Spr 79
Lawrence, Adele
  A virgin doesn't have to say no. Var spec 5:105-11 Mid-Spr 79
Scuba sex [letter]. Var spec 5:157 Mid-Spr 79

FEMALE MASTURBATION
  See also Ben-Wa Balls
    Dildos
    Hairdryers
    Shower sprays
    Vibrators

FEMALE MASTURBATION—PERSONAL ACCOUNTS
Bedpost fun [letter]. Var spec 5:102-3 Mid-Spr 79
Cold comfort [letter]. Var spec 5:103 Mid-Spr 79
Phillips, Kate
  Ben Wa balls: a woman's secret delight. Var spec 5:96-9 Mid-Spr 79
Virgin by choice [letter]. Var spec 5:112 Mid-Spring 79

FEMALE ORGASM
Crown, Sandra
  Female sexual fulfillment: what it really means. Hum Dig 3-1: 39-45 Jan 79
Dailey, Jan
  Women and orgasm: how to achieve it no matter what. Sexol 46-2: 10-18 Oct 79
Holaday, Robert
  Frigidity: the causes & the cures. Hum Dig 3-1:23-7 Jan 79

FEMALE ORGASM—PERSONAL ACCOUNTS
Can't reach climax [letter]. Sexol 46-2:72-3 Oct 79

FEMALE PROSTITUTES—PERSONAL ACCOUNTS
Finley, Theresa
  Transsexual call girl. Var spec 5:127-31 Mid-Spr 79

FEMINIST-LESBIAN ARCHIVES. See LESBIAN-FEMINIST ARCHIVES.

FETISHES. See BALDNESS FETISH; DIAPER FETISH: PANTY FETISH; PILLOW FETISH; RUBBER FETISH.

FICTION. See EROTIC FICTION; GAY FICTION; SHORT STORIES.

FILM ACTORS. See EROTIC FILM ACTORS.

FILM REVIEWS. See EROTIC FILMS—REVIEWS; GAY FILMS—REVIEWS.

FILMS, ENEMA. See ENEMA FILMS.

FILMS, EROTIC. See EROTIC FILMS.

FILMS, GAY. See GAY FILMS.

Finley, Theresa
  Transsexual call girl. Var spec 5:127-31 Mid-Spr 79

Fisher, Pete
  Special teachers/special boys. 1979.
  Review (Scott Jones): Gay Sun 40/41:32 Sum/Fall 79

FIST-FUCKING—PERSONAL ACCOUNTS
Califia, Pat
  Pleasure/pain and power—a Lesbian's view. Var spec 5:56-65 Mid-Spr 79

Fletcher, Sheila
  Quarry [poem]. SYOL 21:10 Oct 78

FLYING SEX. See AIRPLANE SEX.

FOURSOMES. See MATE-SWAPPING; SWINGING.

Friedman, Leslie
Sex role stereotyping in the mass media: an annotated bibliography. 1974.
　　Review (Scott C. McDonald): J Homo 4-2:192-4 Win 78

Friel, T.
Transvestite marriage: hubby was wigged-put on women's clothes. Fetish T 64:4-6+

Friendly, Suzanne
I can be very friendly. Pillow T 3-6:8-10 Sep 79

FRIGIDITY
See also Impotence
Holaday, Robert
　　Frigidity: the causes & the cures. Hum Dig 3-1:23-7 Jan 79

"FUCKING." See ANAL SEX; BESTIALITY; HETEROSEXUAL INTERCOURSE; HOMOSEXUAL INTERCOURSE.

FULFILLING YOUNG CUPS (FILM)
Neuhaus, Manny
　　Kennel ration raunch [review of Fulfilling young cups]. Screw 548:23 Sep 3, 79

Gambill, Sue
Opening, a short story. SYOL 21:7-8 Oct 78

GAY ARCHIVES
See also Lesbian-Feminist archives
Monahan, Jim
　　Considerations in the organization of Gay archives. Gay Insurg 4/5:8-10 Spr 79

GAY CHILDREN
Morin, Stephen F.
　　"The Gay movement and the rights of children." J of Social Issues. 1978.
　　Review (Daniel Tsang): Gay Insurg 4/5:48 Spr 79

GAY FATHERS—PERSONAL ACCOUNTS
Latham, Jack Purdom
　　Tender mornings: progress of a faggot father. Gay Sun 40/41: 10-12 Sum/Fall 79

GAY FICTION
Gambill, Sue
　　Opening, a short story. SYOL 21:7-8 Oct 78

GAY FICTION—BIBLIOGRAPHY
McDonnell, Linda
　　Bibliography: 20th Century American Lesbian novels. SYOL 21:16 Oct 78

GAY FICTION—HISTORY AND CRITICISM—REVIEWS
Austen, Roger
　　Playing the game: the homosexual novel in America. 1977.
　　Review (Byrne R. S. Fone): J Homo 4-2:195-200 Win 78

GAY FICTION—REVIEWS
•Christian, Paula
　　Edge of twilight. 1959.
　　This side of love. 1963.
　　Reviews (S.C.): SYOL 21:22 Oct 78
•Curzon, Daniel
　　Among the carnivores. 1979.
　　Review (Scott Jones): Gay Sun 40/41:32 Sum/Fall 79
•Fisher, Pete
　　Special teachers/special boys. 1979.
　　Review (Scott Jones): Gay Sun 40/41:32 Sum/Fall 79
•Hamilton, Wallace
　　David at Olivet. 1979
　　Review (Scott Jones): Gay Sun 40/41:32 Sum/Fall 79
•Kramer, Larry
　　Faggots. 1978.
　　Review (Larry Puchall): Gay Sun 40/41:34 Sum/Fall 79
•Titkin, Carl
　　Ron. 1979.
　　Review (Scott Jones): Gay Sun 40/41:32 Sum/Fall 79
•Watmough, David

No more into the garden. 1978.
Review (Scott Jones): Gay Sun 40/41:32 Sum/Fall 79
•White, Edmund
Nocturnes for the King of Naples. 1978.
Review (Scott Jones): Gay Sun 40/41:32 Sum/Fall 79

GAY FILMS—REVIEWS
Cruikshank, Peg
Notes on two films: Julia and Word is out. SYOL 21:11 Oct 78

GAY LIBERATION MOVEMENT —BIBLIOGRAPHY
Katz, Jonathan
Gay men, Lesbians, and Socialism: a bibliography of some relevant books, pamphlets, essays, periodicals, and news items. Gay Insurg 4/5:51-6 Spr 79

GAY LIBERATION MOVEMENT —BOOK REVIEWS
•Crew, Louie
The Gay academic. 1978.
Review (Jim Monahan): Gay Insurg 4/5:43-7 Spr 79
•Gay Theory Work Group of the Movement for a New Society
Gay oppression and liberation or, Homophobia: its causes and cure. 1977.
Review (Marc Killinger): Gay Insurg 4/5:37-42 Spr 79

GAY LIBERATION MOVEMENT —LIBRARY RESOURCES
Tsang, Daniel
The Gay press. Gay Insurg 4/5: 18-21 Spr 79

GAY LITERATURE
See also Gay Fiction
Gay poetry

GAY LITERATURE—HISTORY AND CRITICISM—BOOK REVIEWS
Leyland, Winston
Now the volcano: an anthology of Latin American Gay literature. 1979.
Review (E. A. Lacey): Gay Sun 40/41:26-31 Sum/Fall 79

GAY LITERATURE—REVIEWS
•Ginsberg, Allen
To Eberhart from Ginsberg; a letter about HOWL. 1976.
Allen Ginsberg journals; early Fifties early Sixties. 1977.
As ever; the collected correspondence of Allen Ginsberg and Neal Cassady. 1977.
Mind breaths; poems 1972-1977. 1977.
Reviews (David Chura): Gay Sun 40/41:15-16 Sum/Fall 79

GAY MEN
See also Gays
Homosexuality

GAY MEN—IDENTITY
Weinberg, Thomas S.
On "doing" and "being" Gay: sexual behavior and homosexual male self-identity. J Homo 4-2:143-56 Win 78

GAY MEN IN NEWS MEDIA
Boston/Boise Committee
Suggestions for media on handling alleged sex "crimes" involving Gay men. Gay Insurg 4/5: 56-9 Spr 79

GAY MEN—PSYCHOLOGY
Bernard, Larry Craig
Androgyny scores of matched homosexual and heterosexual males. J Homo 4-2:169-78 Win 78
Ross, Michael W.
The relationship of perceived societal hostility, conformity, and psychological adjustment in homosexual males. J Homo 4-2:157-68 Win 78
Weinberg, Thomas S.
On "doing" and "being" Gay: sexual behavior and homosexual male self-identity. J Homo 4-2:143-56 Win 78

GAY MEN—SEXUALITY
See also Anal sex
Analingus
Boy love
Fellatio
Fist-fucking
Homosexuality
Male prostitutes
Witomski, T. R.
Beyond the last taboo. Var spec 5:136-40 Mid-Spr 79

GAY PACIFISTS
Mager, Don
Dr. Magnus Hirschfeld as socialist pacifist thinker. Gay Insurg 4/5:2-8 Spr 79

GAY PERIODICALS—BIBLIOGRAPHY—UNION LISTS
Tsang, Daniel.
The Gay press. Gay Insurg 4/5:18-21 Spr 79

GAY POETRY
Antler
Poems. Gay Sun 40/41:36 Summer/Fall 79
Arrizabalaga y Prado, Leonardo de
Song without words [poem]. Gay Sun 40/41:35 Sum/Fall 79
Beame, Jeffery
Tonight desire has a man in it [poem]. Gay Sun 40/41:37 Sum/Fall 79
Blakeston, Oswell
The graveyard [poem]. Gay Sun 40/41:37 Sum/Fall 79
Chadwick, Jerah
Making it new [poem]. Gay Sun 40/41:35 Sum/Fall 79
Goldberg, Arleen
Bow/river: Banff 1977 [poem]. SYOL 21:9 Oct 78
Hawley, Ellen
The repeal of the St. Paul Gay Rights Ordinance/A variation on the repeal of the St. Paul Gay Rights Ordinance [poems]. SYOL 21:2 Oct 78
Peterson, Marcia A.
Today [poem]. SYOL 21:12 Oct 78
Reith, Kimi
Being a dyke [poem]. SYOL 21:2 Oct 78
Shurin, Aaron
Return to Delphi [poem]. Gay Sun 40/41:40 Sum/Fall 79
Stein, Diane
Lets just let it go at that [poem]. SYOL 21:3 Oct 78
When it hit the fan [poem]. SYOL 21:3 Oct 78
Why I get fired again again [poem]. SYOL 21:3 Oct 78
Trifonov, Gennady
Three poems. Gay Sun 40/41:12 Sum/Fall 79
Wallner, S.
Kathleen [poem]. SYOL 21:10 Oct 78

GAY POETRY—REVIEWS
•Abbott, Steve
Wrecked hearts; raw poetry
Review (R. Daniel Evans): Gay Sun 40/41:35 Sum/Fall 79
•Kelly, Dennis
Chicken; boy love poems. 1979.
Review (Charley Shively): Gay Sun 40/41:9 Sum/Fall 79
•Kirmani, Awhaduddin
Heart's witness. 1978.
Review (Winston Leyland): Gay Sun 40/41:33 Sum/Fall 79
•Mariah, Paul
This light will spread: selected poems 1960-1975. 1978.
Review (Steve Abbott): Gay Sun 40/41:33 Sum/Fall 79
•Orlovsky, Peter
Clean asshole poems & smiling vegetable songs. 1978.
Review (Charles Shively): Gay Sun 40/41:15 Sum/Fall 79
•Rimbaud, Arthur
Rimbaud/Verlaine: a lover's cock. 1979.
Review (Arthur William Rudolph): Gay Sun 40/41:38 Sum/Fall 79
•Ronan, Richard
Flowers; poems. 1978.
Review (E. A. Lacey): Gay Sun 40/41:32 Sum/Fall 79

GAY POETS—INTERVIEWS
Duncan, Robert
Interview. Gay Sun 40/41:1-8 Sum/Fall 79

GAY PRISONERS—PERSONAL ACCOUNTS
Williams, Dalton Lloyd
Prison sex at age 16; County Jail: a true incident. Gay Sun 40/41:14 Sum/Fall 79

GAY RESEARCH—BOOK REVIEWS
Crew, Louie
The Gay academic. 1978.
Review (Jim Monahan): Gay Insurg 4/5:43-7 Spr 79

GAY RIGHTS
Sullivan, Timothy J.
Attempted repeals of Gay Rights ordinances: the facts. Sex L Rptr 4-4:61+ Oct/Dec 78

GAY RIGHTS—POETRY
Hawley, Ellen
The repeal of the St. Paul Gay Rights Ordinance/A variation on the repeal of the St. Paul Gay Rights Ordinance [poems]. SYOL 21:2 Oct 78

GAY SOCIALISM—BIBLIOGRAPHY
Katz, Jonathan
Gay men, Lesbians, and Socialism: a bibliography of some relevant books, pamphlets, essays, periodicals, and news items. Gay Insurg 4/5:51-6 Spr 79

GAY SOCIALISTS
Mager, Don
Dr. Magnus Hirschfeld as socialist pacifist thinker. Gay Insurg 4/5:2-8 Spr 79

GAY SOLDIERS—BOOK REVIEWS
Gibson, E. Lawrence
Get off my ship. 1978.
Review (Daniel Tsang): Gay Insurg 4/5:47 Spr 79

Gay Theory Work Group of the Movement for a new Society
Gay oppression and liberation or, Homophibia: its causes and cure. 1977.
Review (Marc Killinger): Gay Insurg 4/5:37-42 Spr 79

GAY WOMEN. See LESBIANS.

GAYS—BIBLIOGRAPHY—REVIEWS
•Bullough, Vern L
An annotated bibliography of homosexuality. 1976.
Review (A. P. M. Coxon): Gay Insurg 4/5:49 Spr 79
•Parker, William
Homosexuality bibliography: Supplement, 1970-1975. 1977.
Review (Daniel Tsang): Gay Insurg 4/5:49 Spr 79

GAYS—HISTORY
See also Homosexuality—History

GAYS—HISTORY—BOOK REVIEWS
Evans, Arthur
Witchcraft and the Gay counterculture. 1978.
Review (Will Inman): Gay Sun 40/41:31-2 Sum/Fall 79

GAYS IN ENCYCLOPEDIAS
SantaVicca, Edmund F.
Evaluating encyclopedias: a framework summary. Gay Insurg 4/5:15-17 Spr 79

GAYS—LANGUAGE—BIBLIOGRAPHY
Hayes, Joseph J.
Language and language behavior of Lesbian women and Gay men: a selected bibliography (Part 1). J Homo 4-2: 201-12 Win 78

GAYS—LATIN AMERICA
Lacey, E. A.
Latin America: myths and real-

ities. Gay Sun 40/41:22-6 Sum/Fall 79

GAYS—LEGAL STATUS, LAWS, ETC.
See also Gay rights
Sodomy law
Appellate court again declares Ohio solicitation law unconstitutional. Sex L Reptr 4-4:64-8 Oct/Dec 78
Sexual preference of Big Brothers may be subject to scrutiny. Sex L Reptr 4-4:74 Oct/Dec 78
Sullivan, Timothy J.
Attempted repeals of Gay Rights ordinances: the facts. Sex L Reptr 4-4:61+ Oct/Dec 78

GAYS—SUBJECT HEADINGS. See SUBJECT HEADINGS—GAYS.

Gersten, Leon
"The fantasy game." Pillow T 3-6:91-3 Sep 79

Gibson, E. Lawrence
Get off my ship. 1978.
Review (Daniel Tsang): Gay Insurg 4/5:47 Spr 79

Ginsberg, Allen
To Eberhart from Ginsberg; a letter about HOWL. 1976.
Allen Ginsberg journals; early Fifties early Sixties. 1977.
Mind breaths; poems 1972-1977. 1977.
As ever; the collected correspondence of Allen Ginsberg and Neal Cassady. 1977.
Reviews (David Chura): Gay Sun 40/41:15-16 Sum/Fall 79

Goldberg, Arleen
Bow/river: Banff 1977 [poem]. SYOL 21:9 Oct 78
A well kept secret [poem]. SYOL 21:21 Oct 78

GREEK CULTURE. See ANAL SEX.

GROUP SEX. See SWINGING; THREESOMES.

HAIR, ARMPIT. See ARMPIT HAIR.

HAIRDRYERS
Home help [letter]. Var spec 5:100-1 Mid-Spr 79

Hamilton, Jack
The Redcoats are coming. Screw 548:18-19 Sep 3, 79

Hamilton, Wallace
David at Olivet. 1979.
Review (Scott Jones): Gay Sun 40/41:32 Sum/Fall 79

HAND-FUCKING. See FIST FUCKING.

HAND HAIRDRYERS. See HAIRDRYERS.

HAND VIBRATORS. See VIBRATORS.

Hawley, Ellen
The repeal of the St. Paul Gay Rights Ordinance/A variation on the repeal of the St. Paul Gay Rights Ordinance [poems]. SYOL 21:2 Oct 78

Hayes, Joseph J.
Language and language behavior of Lesbian women and Gay men: a selected bibliography (Part 1). J Homo 4-2:201-12 Win 78

Hellander, Martha
On edge [poem]. SYOL 21:12 Oct 78

HETEROSEXUAL INTERCOURSE
See also Afterplay
Anal sex
Coital positions
Erections
Bliss, K. D.
Beating the short time Charlie blues. Resp 6-9:27-31 Oct 79

Karlen, Arno
   Who's on top? The sexual conflict people don't talk about. Sexol 46-2:24-9 Oct 79

Shore, Jeannie
   How to cope with those first-night jitters. Hum Dig 3-1:9-12 Jan 79
   That size question [letter]. Hum Dig 3-1:66-7 Jan 79

HETEROSEXUAL INTERCOURSE—PERSONAL ACCOUNTS

Borchette, Suzanne
   A night in Central Park. Var spec 5:86-91 Mid-Spr 79

Cooperstock, David
   The joys of sex without an erection. Var spec 5:12-17 Mid-Spr 79

Crown, Sandra
   Female sexual fulfillment: what it really means. Hum Dig 3-1:39-45 Jan 79
   Delectable delirium [letter]. Var spec 5:162 Mid-Spr 79
   Jingle balls [letter]. Var spec 5:159 Mid-Spr 79
   Joy stick [letter]. Var spec 5:94-5 Mid-Spr 79
   One-legged [letter]. Hum Dig 3-1:57-9 Jan 79
   A rare virgin [letter]. Var spec 5:114 Mid-Spr 79
   Snow games [letter]. Var spec 5:94 Mid-Spr 79

Stahl, Jerry
   A way to find ecstasy; after a week of yoga, fasting and silence, a man and a woman experience supreme bliss at the edge of a precipice. Var spec 5:6-11 Mid-Spr 79

HETEROSEXUAL MEN—PSYCHOLOGY

Bernard, Larry Craig
   Androgyny scores of matched homosexual and heterosexual males. J Homo 4-2:169-78 Win 78

HETEROSEXUALITY

Deni, Laura
   Why nice girls finish last. Pillow T 3-6:16-21+ Sep 79

Pomeroy, Wardell B.
   What heterosexuals can learn from homosexuals. Sexol 46-2:36-8 Oct 79

HIRSCHFELD, MAGNUS

Mager, Don
   Dr. Magnus Hirschfeld as a socialist pacifist thinker. Gay Insurg 4/5:2-8 Spr 79

Hodges, Parker
   That misunderstood erogenous zone; the nipple—a powerful source of erotic pleasure in both men and women—is largely unexplored. Sexol 46-2:30-4 Oct 79

Hoffman, Lisa
   A bisexual wedding; interview and photos. Porn film star Marc Stevens marries transsexual model Jill Monro. Var spec 5:18-27 Mid-Spr 79

Hoffman, Susan
   A meditation on Adrienne Rich's Splittings [poem]. SYOL 21:5 Oct 78

Holaday, Robert
   Frigidity: the causes & the cures. Hum Dig 3-1:23-7 Jan 79

Holt, Miranda
   Part-time marriage: a new way to have your cake and eat it too. Hum Dig 3-1:19-22 Jan 79

HOMOPHOBIA—BOOK REVIEWS

Gay Theory Work Group of the Movement For A New Society
   Gay oppression and liberation or, Homophobia: its causes and cure. 1977.
   Review (Marc Killinger): Gay Insurg 4/5:37-42 Spr 79

HOMOPHOBIA IN LIBRARIANSHIP

Berman, Sanford
   Gay access: new approaches in

cataloging. Gay Insurg 4/5:14-15 Spr 79

HOMOPHOBIA IN NEWS MEDIA
Boston/Boise Committee
Suggestions for media on handling alleged sex "crimes" involving Gay men. Gay Insurg 4/5:56-9 Spr 79

HOMOPHOBIA IN THE ARMED FORCES—BOOK REVIEWS
Gibson, E. Lawrence
Get off my ship. 1978.
Review (Daniel Tsang): Gay Insurg 4/5:47 Spr 79

HOMOSEXUAL CHILDREN. See GAY CHILDREN.

HOMOSEXUAL INTERCOURSE
See also Afterplay
Anal sex
Coital positions
Erections
Fist-fucking

HOMOSEXUAL INTERCOURSE—PERSONAL ACCOUNTS
Bisexual husband [letter]. Var spec 5:28-9 Mid-Spr 79

HOMOSEXUAL MEN. See GAY MEN.

HOMOSEXUAL WOMEN. See LESBIANS.

HOMOSEXUALITY
See also Bisexuals
Boy love
Gay men
Gays
Homosexual intercourse
Lesbians
Pomeroy, Wardell B.
What heterosexuals can learn from homosexuals. Sexol 46-2:36-8 Oct 79

HOMOSEXUALITY—BIBLIOGRAPHY—REVIEWS
•Bullough, Vern L.
An annotated bibliography of homosexuality. 1976.
Review (A. P. M. Coxon): Gay Insurg 4/5:49 Spr 79
Review (William Parker): J Homo 4-2:185-92 Win 78
•Parker, William
Homosexuality bibliography: Supplement, 1970-1975. 1977.
Review (Daniel Tsang): Gay Insurg 4/5:49 Spr 79

HOMOSEXUALITY—HISTORY
See also Gays—History
Kennedy, Hubert C.
The case for James Mills Peirce. J Homo 4-2:79-84 Win 78

HOMOSEXUALITY—HISTORY—BOOK REVIEWS
Dover, Kenneth J.
Greek homosexuality. 1978.
Review (Arthur William Rudolph): Gay Sun 40/41:33-4 Sum /Fall 79

HOMOSEXUALITY IN ENCYCLOPEDIAS
SantaVicca, Edmund F.
Evaluating encyclopedias: a framework summary. Gay Insurg 4/5:15-17 Spr 79

HOMOSEXUALS. See GAYS.

"HOOKERS." See FEMALE PROSTITUTES; MALE PROSTITUTES.

HUMILIATION. See BONDAGE AND DISCIPLINE; SADOMASOCHISM.

HYGIENE, SEXUAL. See SEXUAL HYGIENE.

IMPOTENCE
Potency problem [letter]. Hum Dig 3-1:83-4 Jan 79

INCEST
See also Brother-sister incest
Father-daughter incest
Mother-son incest

Love thy mother [letter]. Hum Dig 3-1:62 Jan 79

INCEST—PERSONAL ACCOUNTS
Secret lovers [letter]. Hum Dig 3-1: 59-60 Jan 79

INFERTILITY
Romeo, Sherry
Infertility. Sexol 46-2:8-9 Oct 79

INTERCOURSE. See ANAL SEX; BESTIALITY; HETEROSEXUAL INTERCOURSE; HOMOSEXUAL INTERCOURSE.

Jackson, Damaris
Dancers in the studio [poem]. SYOL 21:4 Oct 78
To the Winter solstice [poem]. SYOL 21:24 Oct 78

Jackson, Martin A.
How color affects your life and love. Pillow T 3-6:77-81+ Sept 79

Jardine, Jack Owen
Oh, you beautiful doll! Var spec 5: 142-7 Mid-Spr 79

"JERKING OFF." See MALE MASTURBATION.

Jolly, Lara
A time of reaping [poem]. SYOL 21:22 Oct 78

Jordon, Flash
Dildonuts [cartoon]. Screw 548:24 -5 Sep 3, 79

JULIA (FILM)
Cruikshank, Peg
Notes on two films: Julia and Word is out. SYOL 21:11 oct 78

Karlen, Arno
Who's on top? The sexual conflict people don't talk about. Sexol 46-2:24-9 Oct 79

Katz, Jonathan
Gay men, Lesbians, and Socialism: a bibliography of some relevant books, pamphlets, essays, periodicals, and news items. Gay Insurg 4/5:51-6 Spr 79

Kelly, Dennis
Chicken; boy love poems. 1979.
Review (Charley Shively): Gay Sun 40/41:9 Sum/Fall 79

Kempler, Jana
A couple takes a chance. Var spec 5:70-81 Mid-Spr 79

Kennedy, Hubert C.
The case for James Mills Peirce. J Homo 4-2:179-84 Win 78

Kirmani, Awhaduddin
Heart's witness; the Sufi quatrains of Awhaduddin Kirmani. 1978.
Review (Winston Leyland): Gay Sun 40/41:33 Sum/Fall 79

Klaskin, Ronnie
The difference between making love and getting fucked. Pillow T 3-6:67-71 Sep 79

Klein, Art
Hello, I am Joe's penis. Pillow T 3-6:82-8 Sep 79

Kramer, Larry
Faggots. 1978.
Review (Larry Puchall): Gay Sun 40/41:34 Sum/Fall 79

Krause, Donna M.
Playing tough [poem]. SYOL 21: 24 Oct 78

Lacey, E. A.
Latin America: myths and realities. Gay Sun 40/41:22-6 Sum/Fall 79

LATEX FETISH. See RUBBER FETISH.

Latham, Jack Purdom
Tender mornings: progress of a faggot father. Gay Sun 40/41:10-12 Sum/Fall 79

LATIN AMERICA
Lacey, E. A.
Latin America: myths and realities. Gay Sun 40/41:22-6 Sum/Fall 79

LATIN AMERICA—BOOK REVIEWS
Leyland, Winston
Now the volcano: an anthology of Latin American Gay literature. 1979.
Review (E. A. Lacey): Gay Sun 40/41:26-31 Sum/Fall 79

Lawrence, Adele
A virgin doesn't have to say no. Var spec 5:105-11 Mid-Spr 79

LAWS, SEX. See SEX LAWS.

LeBlanc, Maryjean
Leaving [story]. SYOL 21:13-14 Oct 78

LESBIAN ALCOHOLICS
Diamond, Deborah L.
Alcohol abuse among Lesbians: a descriptive study. J Homo 4-2:123-42 Win 78

LESBIAN-FEMINIST ARCHIVES
Nestle, Joan
Radical archiving: a Lesbian Feminist perspective. Gay Insurg 4/5:10-12 Spr 79

LESBIAN HERSTORY ARCHIVES
Nestle, Joan
Radical archiving: a Lesbian Feminist perspective. Gay Insurg 4/5:10-12 Spr 79

LESBIAN MOTHERS—FICTION
Gambill, Sue
Opening, a short story. SYOL 21:7-8 Oct 78

LESBIANS
See also Gays
Homosexuality
Women's sexuality

LESBIANS—DIARIES
McNaron, Toni
Excerpts from a New York journal, April 1978. SYOL 21:18-20 Oct 78

LESBIANS—FICTION—BIBLIOGRAPHY
McDonnell, Linda
Bibliography: 20th Century American Lesbian novels. SYOL 21:16 Oct 78

LESBIANS—IDENTITY
Coming out [letter]. Hum Dig 3-1:68-70 Jan 79

LESBIANS IN FICTION
Christian, Paula
Edge of twilight. 1959.
This side of love. 1963.
Reviews (S.C.): SYOL 21:22 Oct 78

LESBIANS—PERSONAL ACCOUNTS
Califia, Pat
Pleasure/pain and power—a Lesbian's view. Var spec 5:56-65 Mid-Spr 79
Catherine, Eleanor
It happened on a train. Var special 5:116-20 Mid-Spr 79
Coming out [letter]. Hum Dig 3-1: 68-70 Jan 79
Craves punishment [letter]. Var spec 5:68-Mid-Spr 79
Double dong [letter]. Var spec 5:101-2 Mid-Spr 79
Spanking lovers [letter]. Var spec 5:66-8 Mid-Spr 79

LESBIANS—POETRY
Goldberg, Arleen
Bow/river: Banff 1977 [poem]. SYOL 21:9 Oct 78
Peterson, Marcia A.
Today [poem]. SYOL 21:12 Oct 78
Reith, Kimi
Being a dyke [poem]. SYOL 21:2 Oct 78
Stein, Diane

Lets just let it go at that [poem]. SYOL 21:3 Oct 78

When it hit the fan [poem]. SYOL 21:3 Oct 78

Why I get fired again again [poem]. SYOL 21:3 Oct 78

Wallner, S.
Kathleen [poem]. SYOL 21:10 Oct 78

LESBIANS—PSYCHOLOGY
Diamond, Deborah L.
Alcohol abuse among Lesbians: a descriptive study. J Homo 4-2:123-42 Win 78

Leyland, Winston
Now the volcano: an anthology of Latin American Gay literature. 1979.
Review (E. A. Lacey): Gay Sun 40/41:26-31 Sum/Fall 79

LIBRARY HOMOPHOBIA. See HOMOPHOBIA IN LIBRARIANSHIP.

LIMERICKS
Moon, Little
Doping it out [illustrated limericks]. Screw 548:9-11 Sep 3, 79

LINGERIE FETISH. See PANTY FETISH.

LUBRICATION, VAGINAL. See VAGINAL LUBRICATION.

McCartney, Nora
How to beat those "not tonight dear, I've got a headache" blues. Hum Dig 3-1:28-31 Jan 79

McDonnell, Linda
Angling [poem]. SYOL 21:9 Oct 78
Bibliography: 20th Century American Lesbian novels. SYOL 21:16 Oct 78

McGregor, Michelle
Viva vibrators! A complete rundown on all the latest vibrators and sex aids. A consumer report for the truly sensual woman. Hum Dig 3-1:50-4 Jan 79

McNaron, Toni
Excerpts from a New York journal, April 1978. SYOL 21:18-20 Oct 78

Mager, Don
Dr. Magnus Hirschfeld as socialist pacifist thinker. Gay Insurg 4/5:2-8 Spr 79

MALE IMPOTENCE. See IMPOTENCE.

MALE MASTURBATION
See also Hairdryers
Sex dolls
Shower sprays
Vibrators

MALE MASTURBATION—PERSONAL ACCOUNTS
An endless source of pleasure [letter]. Var spec 5:148-9 Mid-Spr 79
Glove love [letter]. Var spec 5:149 Mid-Spr 79
Helping hand [letter]. Hum Dig 3-1:73-4 Jan 79
Light my fire [letter]. Var spec 5:158-9 Mid-Spr 79
Man's ingenuity [letter]. Var spec 5:156-7 Mid-Spr 79

MALE PROSTITUTES
Male prostitutes [letter]. Var spec 5:133-4 Mid-Spr 79
Urban tragedy [letter]. Sexol 46-2:61 Oct 79

MALE PROSTITUTES—PERSONAL ACCOUNTS
Advice from a male prostitute [letter]. Var spec 5:132-5 Mid-Spr 79

MAN/BOY LOVE. See BOY LOVE.

Mariah, Paul
This light will spread: selected poems 1960-1975. 1978.

Review (Steve Abbott): Gay Sun 40/41:34 Sum/Fall 79

MARRIAGE
See also Extramarital relations
Mate-swapping
Part-time marriage
Hoffman, Lisa
A bisexual wedding; interview and photos. Porn film star Marc Stevens marries transsexual model Jill Monro. Var spec 5:18-27 Mid-Spr 79

MARRIAGE—FICTION
LeBlanc, Maryjean
Leaving [story]. SYOL 21:13-14 Oct 78

MARRIAGE, PART-TIME. See PART-TIME MARRIAGE.

Marshall, Thurgood
Mr. Justice Marshall on sexual privacy rights. Sex L Reptr 4-4: 75-7 Oct/Dec 78

MASOCHISM. See SADOMASOCHISM.

MASSAGE
Altman, Carole
Too tense for love? Try these relaxation techniques that work! Sexol 46-2:39-43 Oct 79

MASSAGE—PERSONAL ACCOUNTS
Facing it [letter]. Sexol 46-2:57 Oct 79

MASTURBATION
See also Female masturbation
Male masturbation
Mutual masturbation
Sex aids

MASTURBATION—PERSONAL ACCOUNTS
Catherine, Eleanor
It happened on a train. Var spec 5:116-20 Mid-Spr 79

Masturbation hints [letter]. Hum Dig 3-1:56 Jan 79

MATE-SWAPPING
See also Swinging

MATE-SWAPPING—PERSONAL ACCOUNTS
Anal fear [letter]. Hum Dig 3-1: 89-90 Jan 79
Bisexual swingers [letter]. Var spec 5:52-4 Mid-Spr 79
Hamilton, Jack
The Redcoats are coming. Screw 548:18-19 Sep 3, 79
Swappers' life style [letter]. Var spec 5:51-2 Mid-Spring 79

MEN, GAY. See GAY MEN.

MEN, HETEROSEXUAL. See HETEROSEXUAL MEN.

MEN PROSTITUTES. See MALE PROSTITUTES.

MENAGE A TROIS. See THREESOMES.

MEN'S MASTURBATION. See MALE MASTURBATION.

MEN'S SEXUALITY. See ERECTIONS; GAY MEN; HETEREOSEXUAL INTERCOURSE; HETEROSEXUAL MEN; HOMOSEXUAL INTERCOURSE; IMPOTENCE; MALE MASTURBATION; MALE PROSTITUTES; MIDDLE-AGED MEN'S SEXUALITY; PENIS; PENIS SIZE; PREMATURE EJACULATION; SENIOR MEN'S SEXUALITY; TRANSSEXUALS; TRANSVESTITES.

MIDDLE-AGED MEN'S SEXUALITY
Thistle, Frank
Are dirty old men really dirty? Pillow T 3-6:28-33 Sep 79

Miller, Kate

Analingus: something special for your lover. Hum Dig 3-1:32-4 Jan 79

Milton, John
Mail order madness. Screw 548:32 Sep 3, 79

MISCONCEPTIONS
Smith, Belle
Sexual myths. Hum Dig 3-1: 46-9 Jan 79

Monahan, Jim
Considerations in the organization of Gay archives. Gay Insurg 4/5:8-10 Spr 79

MONRO, JILL
Hoffman, Lisa
A bisexual wedding; interview and photos. Porn film star Marc Stevens marries transsexual model Jill Monro. Var spec 5:18-27 Mid-Spr 79

Moon, Little
Doping it out [illustrated limericks]. Screw 548:9-11 Sep 3, 79

Moos, Kate
Eggs, for Janis [poem]. SYOL 21:12 Oct 78
The seer [poem]. SYOL 21:12 Oct 78
To Joseph [poem]. SYOL 21:10 Oct 78

Morin, Stephen F.
"The Gay movement and the rights of children." J of Social Issues. 1978.
Review (Daniel Tsang): Gay Insurg 4/5:48 Spr 79

MOTHER-SON INCEST
Love thy mother [letter]. Hum Dig 3-1:62 Jan 79

MOUTH PLAY—PERSONAL ACCOUNTS
Facing it [letter]. Sexol 45-2:57 Oct 79

MOVIE ACTORS. *See* EROTIC FILM ACTORS.

MUSEUM SEX—PERSONAL ACCOUNTS
The balcony [letter]. Var spec 5:121-2 Mid-Spr 79

MUTUAL MASTURBATION—PERSONAL ACCOUNTS
The first time [letter]. Var spec 5:112-13 Mid-Spr 79

Nestle, Joan
Radical archiving: a Lesbian Feminist perspective. Gay Insurg 4/5:10-12 Spr 79

Neuhaus, Manny
Bare facts. Screw 548:13 Sep 3, 79
Kennel ration raunch [review of Fulfilling young cups]. Screw 548:23 Sep 3, 79

NEW AGE—BOOK REVIEWS
Satin, Mark
New Age politics, healing self and society; the emerging new alternative to Marxism and Liberalism. 1978.
Review (Mitch Walker): Gay Sun 40/41:35 Sum/Fall 79

NEWS MEDIA GUIDELINES
Boston/Boise Committee
Suggestions for media on handling alleged sex "crimes" involving Gay men. Gay Insurg 4/5: 56-9 Spr 79

Nichols, D. W.
A boy lover's perspective; D. W. Nichols interviewed by Daniel Tsang, Part II. Gay Insurg 4/5: 25-36 Spr 79

NIPPLE PLAY
Hodges, Parker
That misunderstood erogenous zone; the nipple—a powerful source of erotic pleasure in both men and women—is largely unexplored. Sexol 46-2:30-4 Oct 79

NUDE BEACHES
   A day at the (nude) beach. Var spec 5:122-3 Mid-Spr 79
   Neuhaus, Manny
      Bare facts. Screw 548:13 Sep 3, 79

OBSCENITY LAW
   Buffalo anti-obscenity ordinance is voided. Sex L Rptr 4-4:63 Oct/Dec 78
   'The Finger' is not an obscene gesture. Sex L Rptr 4-4:77 Oct/Dec 78
   Obscenity 'Scienter Test' is subject of dispute. Sex L Rptr 4-4:80 Oct/Dec 78
   Supreme Court rules broadcasters use of indecent language may be regulated. Sex L Rptr 4-4:62-3 Oct/Dec 78

OFFICE SEX
   Gersten, Leon
      "The fantasy game." Pillow T 3-6: 91-3 Sep 79

OLD PEOPLE'S SEXUALITY. See SENIORS' SEXUALITY.

ORAL SEX. See ANALINGUS; CUNNILINGUS; FELLATIO; MOUTH PLAY.

ORGASM, FEMALE. See FEMALE ORGASM.

"ORIENTAL" LOVE BALLS. See BEN-WA BALLS.

Orlovsky, Peter
   Clean asshole poems & smiling vegetable songs. 1978.
      Review (Charles Shively): Gay Sun 40/41:15 Sum/Fall 79

OVER-60 SEXUALITY. See SENIORS' SEXUALITY.

PACIFISTS, GAY. See GAY PACIFISTS.

PAGE, BETTY

Stryker, Rod
   On the rack. Fetish T 64:12-13

PANTY FETISH—PERSONAL ACCOUNTS
   Kinky craftsmanship [letter]. Fetish T 64:9
   Light my fire [letter]. Var spec 5:158-9 Mid-Spr 79

PARENTING
   Turnabout [letter]. Sexol 46-2:53-4 Oct 79

Park, R. L.
   Bondage on the boob tube. Fetish T 64:11

Parker, William
   Homosexuality bibliography: Supplement, 1970-1975. 1977.
      Review (Daniel Tsang): Gay Insurg 4/5:49 Spr 79

PART-TIME MARRIAGE
   Holt, Miriam
      Part-time marriage: a new way to have your cake and eat it too. Hum Dig 3-1:19-22 Jan 79

PEDERASTY. See BOY LOVE.

PEDOPHILIA.
   See also Boy love
   Incestuous seeker [letter]. Hum Dig 3-1:81-3 Jan 79

PEIRCE, JAMES MILLS
   Kennedy, Hubert C.
      The case for James Mills Peirce. J Homo 4-2:179-84 Win 78

PENIS
   See also Circumcision
            Erections
            Impotence
            Premature ejaculation

PENIS—ANECDOTES, SATIRE
   Klein, Art
      Hello, I am Joe's penis. Pillow T 3-6:82-8 Sep 79

PENIS SIZE
Hoffman, Lisa
A bisexual wedding; interview and photos. Porn film star Marc Stevens marries transsexual model Jill Monro. Var spec 5:18-27 Mid-Spr 79
It's not the size [letter]. Sexol 46-2: 59-60 Oct 79
That size question [letter]. Hum Dig 3-1:66-7 Jan 79

PERIODICALS, EROTIC. See EROTIC PERIODICALS.

PERIODICALS, GAY. See GAY PERIODICALS.

Perkowski, Donald
A flesh start: video vice. Screw 548:17 Sep 3, 79

PERSONAL ADVERTISEMENTS
Bonner, T. Pete
Playing the personals. Resp 6-9: 32-8 Oct 79

Peterson, Marcia A.
Today [poem]. SYOL 21:12 Oct 78

Phillips, Kate
Ben-Wa balls: a woman's secret delight. Var spec 5:96-9 Mid-Spr 79

PILLOW FETISH
Pillow talk [letter]. Var spec 5:156 Spr 79

POETRY, See GAY POETRY; LIMERICKS; WOMEN'S POETRY.

Pomeroy, Wardell B.
What heterosexuals can learn from homosexuals. Sexol 46-2:36-8 Oct 79

POMPEII
Brock, Paul
Pompeii: the first city of sexual freedom. A look at the true meaning of Bacchanalia. Sexol 46-2:19-22 Oct 79

Poole, Tom
How to turn on a reluctant lover. Pillow T 3-6:72-5 Sep 79

"PORN" FILM ACTORS. See EROTIC FILM ACTORS.

"PORN" FILMS. See EROTIC FILMS.

"PORN" MAGAZINES. See EROTIC PERIODICALS.

"PORNOGRAPHY," CHILD. See CHILD "PORNOGRAPHY."

POSITIONS, COITAL. See COITAL POSITIONS.

PREJUDICE AGAINST GAYS. See HOMOPHOBIA.

PREMATURE EJACULATION
Bliss, K. D.
Beating the short time Charlie blues. Resp 6-9:27-31 Oct 79

Prendergast, William E.
The sex offender: how to spot him before it's too late. Sexol 46-2: 46-51 Oct 79

PRISON SEX—PERSONAL ACCOUNTS
Williams, Dalton Lloyd
Prison sex at age 16; County Jail: a true incident. Gay Sun 40/41:14 Sum/Fall 79

PRIVACY RIGHTS. See SEXUAL PRIVACY RIGHTS.

PROSTITUTES, CHILD. See CHILD PROSTITUTES.

PROSTITUTES, FEMALE. See FEMALE PROSTITUTES.

PROSTITUTES, MALE. See MALE PROSTITUTES.

PSYCHOLOGY OF GAY MEN. See GAY MEN—PSYCHOLOGY.

PSYCHOLOGY OF HETEROSEXUAL MEN. See HETEROSEXUAL MEN—PSYCHOLOGY.

PSYCHOLOGY OF LESBIANS. See LESBIANS—PSYCHOLOGY.

PSYCHOLOGY OF SEX. See SEXUAL PSYCHOLOGY.

PSYCHOLOGY, SEXUAL. See SEXUAL PSYCHOLOGY.

PUBIS SHAVING
Double dong [letter]. Var spec 5:101-2 Mid-Spr 79

PUNISHMENT. See BONDAGE AND DISCIPLINE; SADOMASOCHISM.

PURITAN (PERIODICAL)
Easy to be hard-core; Screw reviews issue no. 4 of the graphic glossy gash mag Puritan. Screw 548:4-7 Sep 3, 79

"PUSSY-EATING." See CUNNILINGUS.

"PUSSY SHAVING." See PUBIS SHAVING.

Radtke, Janel
Consider the possibilities [poem]. SYOL 21:15 Oct 78

RAPE FANTASIES
Female fantasy [letter]. Var spec 5:40 Mid-Spr 79
Rape fantasy [letter]. Var spec 5:38 Mid-Spr 79

RAPISTS
See also Sex offenders

RAPISTS—PERSONAL ACCOUNTS

Dean, Charles
Reflections of a rapist. Sexol 46-2:44-5 Oct 79

Reith, Kimi
Being a dyke [poem]. SYOL 21:2 Oct 78

RELAXATION
Altman, Carole
Too tense for love? Try these relaxation techniques that work! Sexol 46-2:39-43 Oct 79
McCartney, Nora
How to beat those 'not tonight dear, I've got a headache' blues. Hum Dig 3-1:28-31 Jan 79

RESTAURANT SEX—PERSONAL ACCOUNTS
Furtive fellatio [letter]. Var spec 5:92-3 Mid-Spr 79

RIGHTS OF CHILDREN. See CHILDREN'S RIGHTS.

RIGHTS OF GAYS. See GAY RIGHTS.

RIGHTS OF SEXUAL PRIVACY. See SEXUAL PRIVACY RIGHTS.

Rimbaud, Arthur
Rimbaud/Verlaine: a lover's cock. 1979.
Review (Arthur William Rudolph): Gay Sun 40/41:38 Sum/Fall 79

"RIMMING." See ANALINGUS.

RIN-NO-TAMA BALLS. See BEN-WA BALLS.

ROLLER-COASTER SEX—PERSONAL ACCOUNTS
Roller-coaster riders [letter]. Var spec 5:93-4 Mid-Spr 79

ROLLER DISCO. See DISCO SKATING.

Romeo, Sherry
Infertility. Sexol 46-2:8-9 Oct 79

Ronan, Richard
　Flowers; poems. 1978.
　　Review (E. A. Lacey): Gay Sun 40/41:32 Sum/Fall 79

Ross, Michael W.
　The relationship of perceived societal hostility, conformity, and psychological adjustment in homosexual males. J Homo 4-2: 157-68 Win 78

RUBBER FETISH
　Stryker, Rod
　　On the rack. Fetish T 64:12-13

S/M. See SADOMASOCHISM.

STD. See VENEREAL DISEASE.

SADISM. See SADOMASOCHISM.

SADOMASOCHISM
　See also Bondage and discipline
　　　　　Fist-fucking
　　　　　Spanking
　　　　　Whipping

SADOMASOCHISM—PERSONAL ACCOUNTS
　Califia, Pat
　　Pleasure/pain and power—a Lesbian's view. Var spec 5:56-65 Mid-Spr 79
　Friendly, Suzanne
　　I can be very friendly. Pillow T 3-6:8-10 Sep 79
　　White slave [letter]. Hum Dig 3-1: 63-6 Jan 79

SADOMASOCHIST FANTASIES
　The captured squaw [letter]. Var spec 5:39-40 Mid-Spr 79

SAN FRANCISCO BAY AREA
　Cozad, William
　　Cruisin' the Bay Area. Resp 6-9:52-6 Oct 79

Santa Vicca, Edmund F.
　Evaluating encyclopedias: a framework summary. Gay Insurg 4/5:15-17 Spr 79

Satin, Mark
　New Age politics, healing self and society; the emerging new alternative to Marxism and Liberalism. 1978.
　　Review (Mitch Walker): Gay Sun 40/41:35 Sum/Fall 79

SAUNA SEX
　The sauna the better [letter]. Sexol 46-2:55-6 Oct 79

"SCAT." See COPROPHILIA.

SCHALLER, JON—INTERVIEWS
　Tsang, Daniel
　　Radical distribution. Gay Insurg 4/5:12-13 Spr 79

"SCREWING." See ANAL SEX; BESTIALITY; HETEROSEXUAL INTERCOURSE; HOMOSEXUAL INTERCOURSE.

SEDUCTION
　Poole, Tom
　　How to turn on a reluctant lover. Pillow T 3-6:72-5 Sep 79

SENIOR MEN'S SEXUALITY
　Thistle, Frank
　　Are dirty old men really dirty? Pillow T 3-6:28-33 Sep 79

SENIORS' SEXUALITY
　Man's ingenuity [letter]. Var spec 5:156-7 Mid-Spr 79

SEX AIDS
　See also Ben-Wa balls
　　　　　Dildos
　　　　　Hairdryers
　　　　　Sex dolls
　　　　　Sex shops
　　　　　Shower sprays
　　　　　Vibrators
　Chalking it up [letter]. Var spec 5: 159-60. Mid-Spr 79
　An endless source of pleasure [let-

ter]. Var spec 5:148-9 Mid-Spr 79
Glove love [letter]. Var spec 5:149 Mid-Spr 79
Jingle balls [letter]. Var spec 5:159 Mid-Spr 79
Little Miss Muffet [letter]. Var spec 5:157-8 Mid-Spr 79

SEX AIDS—CATALOGS
Stryker, Rod
On the rack. Fetish T 64:12-13

SEX AIDS—EVALUATION
Milton, John
Mail order madness. Screw 548:32 Sep 3, 79

SEX AND LAW. *See* SEX LAWS.

SEX AND URINATION. *See* "WET" SEX.

SEX COUNSELING AND THERAPY
Bliss, K. D.
Beating the short time Charlie blues. Resp 6-9:27-31 Oct 79
Dailey, Jan
Women and orgasm: how to achieve it no matter what. Sexol 46-2:10-18 Oct 79
Holaday, Robert
Frigidity: the causes & the cures. Hum Dig 3-1:23-7 Jan 79

SEX CRIMES IN NEWS MEDIA
Boston/Boise Committee
Suggestions for media on handling alleged sex "crimes" involving Gay men. Gay Insurg 4/5:56-9 Spr 79

SEX DOLLS
Jardine, Jack Owen.
Oh, you beautiful doll! Var spec 5:142-7 Mid-Spr 79

SEX FILMS. *See* EROTIC FILMS.

SEX HYGIENE. *See* SEXUAL HYGIENE.

SEX IN AIRPLANES. *See* AIRPLANE SEX.

SEX IN CABS. *See* TAXICAB SEX.

SEX IN CARRIAGES. *See* CARRIAGE SEX.

SEX IN ELEVATORS. *See* ELEVATOR SEX.

SEX IN MUSEUMS. *See* MUSEUM SEX.

SEX IN OFFICES. *See* OFFICE SEX.

SEX IN PRISON. *See* PRISON SEX.

SEX IN RESTAURANTS. *See* RESTAURANT SEX.

SEX IN RETAIL STORES. *See* STORE SEX.

SEX IN SAUNAS. *See* SAUNA SEX.

SEX IN STORES. See STORE SEX.

SEX IN TAXICABS. *See* TAXICAB SEX.

SEX IN THE SNOW. *See* SNOW SEX.

SEX IN THEATERS. *See* THEATER SEX.

SEX IN TRAINS. *See* TRAIN SEX.

SEX IN WATER. *See* UNDERWATER SEX.

SEX LAWS
See also Birth control—Laws and regulations
Child molesting—Laws and regulations
Gays—Legal status, laws, etc.

Obscenity law
Sexual privacy rights
Sodomy law
Solicitation law
Youth Liberation
　Children and sex: a Youth Liberation view. Gay Insurg 4/5: 22-4 Spr 79

SEX OFFENDERS
See also Rapists
Prendergast, William E.
　The sex offender: how to spot him before it's too late. Sexol 46-2:46-51 Oct 79

SEX ON ELEVATORS. See ELEVATOR SEX.

SEX ON ROLLER-COASTERS. See ROLLER-COASTER SEX.

SEX ON TRAINS. See TRAIN SEX.

SEX PERIODICALS. See EROTIC PERIODICALS.

SEX PSYCHOLOGY. See SEXUAL PSYCHOLOGY.

SEX ROLE IN MASS MEDIA—BIBLIOGRAPHY—REVIEWS
Friedman, Leslie
Sex role stereotyping in the mass media: an annotated bibliography. 1974.
　Review (Scott C. McDonald): J Homo 4-2:192-4 Win 78

SEX SHOPS
　Double dong [letter]. Var spec 5:101-2 Mid-Spr 79

SEX SHOWS
See also Burlesque shows
　　　　　Erotic films
Friendly, Suzanne
　I can be very friendly. Pillow T 3-6:8-10 Sep 79

SEX THERAPY. See SEX COUNSELING AND THERAPY.

SEX TOYS. See SEX DOLLS.

SEX UNDER WATER. See UNDERWATER SEX.

SEX WITH ANIMALS. See BESTIALITY.

SEXISM IN MASS MEDIA—BIBLIOGRAPHY—REVIEWS
Friedman, Leslie
Sex role stereotyping in the mass media: an annotated bibliography. 1974.
　Review (Scott C. McDonald): J Homo 4-2:192-4 Win 78

SEXUAL AIDS. See SEX AIDS.

SEXUAL DISORDERS
See also Frigidity
　　　　　Impotence
　　　　　Premature ejaculation
　　　　　Sex counseling and therapy
Dailey, Jan
　Women and orgasm: how to achieve it no matter what. Sexol 46-2:10-18 Oct 79
McCartney, Nora
　How to beat those 'not tonight dear, I've got a headache' blues. Hum Dig 3-1:28-31 Jan 79

SEXUAL DISORDERS—PERSONAL ACCOUNTS
　Can't reach climax [letter]. Sexol 46-2:72-3 Oct 79
　Painful intercourse [letter]. Sexol 46-2:79-80 Oct 79

SEXUAL ETHICS
Klaskin, Ronnie
　The difference between making love and getting fucked. Pillow T 3-6:67-71 Sep 79

SEXUAL FANTASIES. See FANTASIES.

SEXUAL FREEDOM. See BACCHANALIA; SWINGING.

SEXUAL HYGIENE
See also Venereal disease

Fighting VD [letter]. Hum Dig 3-1:97
Urinating into the vagina [letter]. Sexol 46-2:76-8 Oct 79

SEXUAL INTERCOURSE. See ANAL SEX; BESTIALITY; HETEROSEXUAL INTERCOURSE; HOMOSEXUAL INTERCOURSE.

SEXUAL MASSAGE. See MASSAGE.

SEXUAL PRIVACY RIGHTS
See also Sodomy law
Marshall, Thurgood
Mr. Justice Marshall on sexual privacy rights. Sex L Rptr 4-4:75-7 Oct/Dec 78

SEXUAL PSYCHOLOGY
See also Fantasies
Gay men—Psychology
Heterosexual men—Psychology
Lesbians—Psychology
Jackson, Martin A.
How color affects your life and love. Pillow T 3-6:77-81+ Sep 79
Klaskin, Ronnie
The difference between making love and getting fucked. Pillow T 3-6:67-71 Sep 79

SEXUALLY TRANSMITTED DISEASE. See VENEREAL DISEASE.

SHAVEN PUBIS. See PUBIS SHAVING.

Shore, Jeannie
How to cope with those first-night jitters. Hum Dig 3-1:9-12 Jan 79

SHORT STORIES
Burleson, Tom
Sensual mind control [story]. Var spec 5:32-7 Mid-Spr 79
Gambill, Sue
Opening, a short story. SYOL 21:7-8 Oct 78

LeBlanc, Maryjean
Leaving [story]. SYOL 21:13-14 Oct 78

SHOWER SPRAYS
Home help [letter]. Var spec 5:100-1 Mid-Spr 79
Shower massage [letter]. Var spec 5:113-14 Mid-Spr 79

Shurin, Aaron
Return to Delphi [poem]. Gay Sun 40/41:40 Sum/Fall 79

SIZE OF BREAST. See BREAST SIZE.

SIZE OF PENIS. See PENIS SIZE.

SIZE OF VAGINA. See VAGINA SIZE.

Small, Larry
Hot licks: a guide to cunnilingus. Resp 6-9:46-50 Oct 79

Smith, Belle
Sexual myths. Hum Dig 3-1:46-9 Jan 79

SNOW SEX
Snow games [letter]. Var spec 5:94 Mid-Spr 79

SOCIALISTS, GAY. See GAY SOCIALISTS.

SODOMY LAW.
Complete text of appellate opinion voiding New Jersey sodomy law. Sex L Rptr 4-4:77-80 Oct/Dec 79

SOLDIERS, GAY. See GAY SOLDIERS.

SOLICITATION LAW
Appellate court again declares Ohio solicitation law unconstitutional. Sex L Rptr 4-4:64-9 Oct/Dec 78

SPANKING
Friel, T.
Transvestite marriage: hubby

was wigged-out on women's clothes. Fetish T 64:4-6+

SPANKING—PERSONAL ACCOUNTS
Craves punishment [letter]. Var spec 5:68 Mid-Spr 79
Kinky craftsmanship [letter]. Fetish T 64:9
Spanking guilt [letter]. Hum Dig 3-1:94-5 Jan 79
Spanking lovers [letter]. Var spec 5:66-8 Mid-Spr 79

SPRAYS, SHOWER. *See* SHOWER SPRAYS.

Stahl, Jerry
A way to find ecstasy; after a week of yoga, fasting and silence, a man and a woman experience supreme bliss at the edge of a precipice. Var spec 5:6-11 Mid-Spr 79

Stein, Diane
Lets just let it go at that [poem]. SYOL 21:3 Oct 78
When it hit the fan [poem]. SYOL 21:3 Oct 78
Why I get fired again again [poem]. SYOL 21:3 Oct 78

STEVENS, MARC
Hoffman, Lisa
A bisexual wedding; interview and photos. Porn film star Marc Stevens marries transsexual model Jil Monro. Var spec 5:18-27 Mid-Spr 79

Stifter, Catherine M.
Abduction/seduction [poem]. SYOL 21:22 Oct 78

STORE SEX—PERSONAL ACCOUNTS
Dress shop romp [letter]. Var spec 5:93 Mid-Spr 79

STORIES. *See* SHORT STORIES

Stryker, Rod
On the rack. Fetish T 64:12-13

SUBJECT HEADINGS—GAYS
Berman, Sanford
Gay access: new approaches in cataloging. Gay Insurg 4/5: 14-15 Spr 79

"SUCKING CUNT." *See* CUNNILINGUS.

"SUCKING OFF." *See* FELLATIO.

Sullivan, Timothy J.
Attempted repeals of Gay Rights ordinances: the facts. Sex L Rptr 4-4:61+ Oct/Dec 78

SWAPPING MATES. *See* MATE-SWAPPING.

SWINGERS' CLUBS
Swinging roundup: the West Coast, the Midwest, the East Coast. Var spec 5:44-50 Mid-Spr 79

SWINGING
See also Mate-swapping
Part-time marriage
Threesomes
Swinging roundup: the West Coast, the Midwest, the East Coast. Var spec 5:44-50 Mid-Spr 79
Watson, Tom
The swinging life. Pillow T 3-6:95-6 Sep 79

SWINGING—PERSONAL ACCOUNTS
A date with eight [letter]. Var spec 5:55 Mid-Spr 79
Here comes the bride [letter]. Var spec 5:54-5 Mid-Spr 79

TAXICAB SEX—PERSONAL ACCOUNTS
Sex on wheels [letter]. Var spec 5:123 Mid-Spr 79

TEENAGERS' SEXUALITY
Accentuate the positive [letter]. Sexol 46-2:54 Oct 79
Adolescent anxieties [letter]. Hum Dig 3-1:77-8 Jan 79

Not quite ready [letter]. Hum Dig 3-1:79-80 Jan 79
Turnabout [letter]. Sexol 46-2: 53-4 Oct 79

TELEVISION BONDAGE AND DISCIPLINE. *See* BONDAGE AND DISCIPLINE IN TELEVISION.

TEMPLE UNIVERSITY LIBRARY
Tsang, Daniel
  The Gay press. Gay Insurg 4/5:18-21 Spr 79

THEATER SEX
Gersten, Leon
  "The fantasy game." Pillow T 3-6:91-3 Sep 79

THERAPY, SEX. *See* SEX COUNSELING AND THERAPY.

Thistle, Frank
  Are dirty old men really dirty? Pillow T 3-6:28-33 Sep 79

THREESOMES
Friel, T.
  Transvestite marriage: hubby was wigged-out on women's clothes. Fetish T 64:4-6+

THREESOMES—PERSONAL ACCOUNTS
Bisexual threesome [letter]. Var spec 5:29 Mid-Spr 79
Crown, Sandra
  Female sexual fulfillment: what it really means. Hum Dig 3-1: 39-45 Jan 79
Friends and lovers [letter]. Var spec 5:83-4 Mid-Spr 79
Kempler, Jana
  A couple takes a chance. Var spec 5:70-81 Mid-Spr 79
Unforgettable melody [letter]. Var spec 5:84-5 Mid-Spr 79
A yacht to learn [letter]. Var spec 5:82 Mid-Spr 79

Titkin, Carl
  Ron. 1979.

Review (Scott Jones): Gay Sun 40/41:32 Sum/Fall 79

TOYS, SEX. *See* SEX DOLLS.

TRAIN SEX
Gersten, Leon
  "The fantasy game." Pillow T 3-6:91-3 Sep 79

TRAIN SEX—PERSONAL ACCOUNTS
Catherine, Eleanor
  It happened on a train. Var spec 5:116-20 Mid-Spr 79
  Chasing the commuter blues [letter]. Var spec 5:123-4 Mid-Spr 79

TRANSSEXUALS—INTERVIEWS
Hoffman, Lisa
  A bisexual wedding; interview and photos. Porn film star Marc Stevens marries transsexual model Jill Monro. Var spec 5:18-27 Mid-Spr 79

TRANSSEXUALS—PERSONAL ACCOUNTS
Finley, Theresa
  Transsexual callgirl. Var spec 5: 127-31 Mid-Spr 79

TRANSVESTITES
Friel, T.
  Transvestite marriage: hubby was wigged-out on women's clothes. Fetish T 64:4-6+

TRANSVESTITES—PERSONAL ACCOUNTS
Shopping tip [letter]. Hum Dig 3-1:74. Jan 79

Trifonov, Gennady
  Three poems. Gay Sun 40/41:12 Sum/Fall 79

Tsang, Daniel
  The Gay press. Gay Insurg 4/5: 18-21 Spr 79
  Radical distribution. Gay Insurg 4/5:12-13 Spr 79

UNDERWATER SEX—PERSONAL ACCOUNTS
Scuba sex [letter]. Var spec 5:157 Mid-Spr 79

URINATION AND SEX. See "WET" SEX.

VD. See VENEREAL DISEASE.

VAGINA SIZE
Large vagina [letter]. Hum Dig 3-1: 80-1 Jan 79

VAGINAL LUBRICATION
See also Cunnilingus
Too dry [letter]. Hum Dig 3-1:94 Jan 79

VENEREAL DISEASE
Fighting VD [letter]. Hum Dig 3-1:97 Jan 79

VIBRATORS
Good vibrations [letter]. Var spec 5:100 Mid-Spr 79
McGregor, Michelle
Viva vibrators! A complete rundown on all the latest vibrators and sex aids. A consumer report for the truly sensual woman. Hum Dig 3-1:50-4 Jan 79
Phillips, Kate
Ben Wa balls: a woman's secret delight. Var spec 5:96-9 Mid-Spr 79

VIDEOTAPE CATALOGS
Your favorite XXX full-length movies are now on video tapes! [advertisement]. Screw 548:8 Sep 3, 79

VIDEOTAPE REVIEWS
Perkowski, Donald
A flesh start: video vice. Screw 548:17 Sep 3, 79

VIRGINITY
Not quite ready [letter]. Hum Dig 3-1: 79-80 Jan 79
The power of virginity [letter]. Sexol 46-2:53 Oct 79

VIRGINITY—PERSONAL ACCOUNTS
A daring debut [letter]. Var spec 5:114-15 Mid-Spr 79
The first time [letter]. Var spec 5:112-13 Mid-Spr 79
Lawrence, Adele
A virgin doesn't have to say no. Var spec 5:105-11 Mid-Spr 79
A rare virgin [letter]. Var spec 5:114 Mid-Spr 79
Virgin by choice [letter]. Var spec 5:112 Mid-Spr 79

Von Eckmann, Erika
A eunuch in every garage [letter]. Fetish T 64:9-10

Wallner, S.
Kathleen [poem]. SYOL 21:10 Oct 78

WATER SPORTS. See "WET" SEX.

WATERPIK SPRAYS. See SHOWER SPRAYS.

Watmough, David
No more into the garden. 1978. Review (Scott Jones): Gay Sun 40/41:32 Sum/Fall 79

Watson, Tom
The swinging life. Pillow T 3-6:95-6 Sep 79

Weinberg, Thomas S.
On "doing" and "being" Gay: sexual behavior and homosexual male self-identity. J Homo 4-2: 143-56 Win 78

"WET" SEX.
Urinating into the vagina [letter]. Sexol 46-2:76-8 Oct 79

WHIPPING—PERSONAL ACCOUNTS
Kinky craftsmanship [letter]. Fetish T 64:9

White, Edmund
Nocturnes for the King of Naples. 1978.
Review (Scott Jones): Gay Sun 40/41:32 Sum/Fall 79

Williams, Dalton Lloyd
Prison sex at age 16; County Jail: a true incident. Gay Sun 40/41:14 Sum/Fall 79

WINTER SEX. See SNOW SEX.

Wiseman, Sarah
Solstice poem. SYOL 21:24 Oct 78

Witomski, T. R.
Beyond the last taboo. Var spec 5:136-40 Mid-Spr 79
Oh, you big brute, you. Pillow T 3-6:12-15 Sep 79

WOMEN, GAY. See LESBIANS.

WOMEN PROSTITUTES. See FEMALE PROSTITUTES.

WOMEN'S ART
Corinne, Tee
The lady who loved horses [graphic]. SYOL 21:24 Oct 78

WOMEN'S EXERCISE. See EXERCISE FOR WOMEN.

WOMEN'S MASTURBATION. See FEMALE MASTURBATION.

WOMEN'S MOVEMENT
Women's Lib 10 years later: is there sex after liberation? [discussion]. Hum Dig 3-1:13-17 Jan 79

WOMEN'S POETRY
See also Lesbians—Poetry
Andrews, Martha
Brief resolution [poem]. SYOL 21:14 Oct 78
Bentley, Caryl B.
A both/and song for the crones [poem]. SYOL 21:5 Oct 78

Colebrook, Val
Inside out [poem]. SYOL 21:24 Oct 78
Strange songs (dreams) [poem]. SYOL 21:15 Oct 78
Fletcher, Sheila
Quarry [poem]. SYOL 21:10 Oct 78
Goldberg, Arleen
A well kept secret [poem]. SYOL 21:21 Oct 78
Hellander, Martha
On edge [poem]. SYOL 21:12 Oct 78
Hoffman, Susan
A meditation on Adrienne Rich's Splittings [poem]. SYOL 21:5 Oct 78
Jackson, Damaris
Dancers in the studio [poem]. SYOL 21:4 Oct 78
To the winter solstice [poem]. SYOL 21:24 Oct 78
Jolly, Lara
A time of reaping [poem]. SYOL 21:22 Oct 78
Krause, Donna M.
Playing tough [poem]. SYOL 21:24 Oct 78
McDonnell, Linda
Angling [poem]. SYOL 21:9 Oct 78
Moos, Kate
Eggs, for Janis [poem]. SYOL 21:12 Oct 78
The seer [poem]. SYOL 21:12 Oct 78
To Joseph [poem]. SYOL 21:10 Oct 78
Radtke, Janel
Consider the possibilities [poem]. SYOL 21:15 Oct 78
Stifter, Catherine M.
Abduction/seduction [poem]. SYOL 21:22 Oct 78
Wiseman, Sarah
Solstice poem. SYOL 21:24 Oct 78

WOMEN'S SEXUALITY
See also Breast feeding
Breasts
Exercise for women

Female masturbation
Female orgasm
Frigidity
Heterosexual intercourse
Homosexual intercourse
Lesbians
Transsexuals
Vagina size
Vaginal lubrication

Crown, Sandra
Female sexual fulfillment: what it really means. Hum Dig 3-1: 39-45 Jan 79

Deni, Laura
Why nice girls finish last. Pillow T 3-6:16-21+ Sep 79

Shore, Jeannie
How to cope with those first-night jitters. Hum Dig 3-1:9-12 Jan 79
Women's Lib 10 years later: is there sex after liberation? [discussion]. Hum Dig 3-1:13-17 Jan 79

WORD IS OUT (FILM)
Cruikshank, Peg
Notes on two films: Julia and Word is out. SYOL 21:11 Oct 78

WORLD WAR I—BOOK REVIEWS
Mager, Don
Dr. Magnus Hirschfeld as socialist pacifist thinker. Gay Insurg 4/5:2-8 Spr 79

YOGA
Stahl, Jerry
A way to find ecstasy; after a week of yoga, fasting and silence, a man and a woman experience supreme bliss at the edge of a precipice. Var spec 5:6-11 Mid-Spr 79

Youth Liberation
Children and sex: A Youth Liberation view. Gay Insurg 4/5:22-4 Spr 79

X-RATED FILMS. *See* EROTIC FILMS.

AUTHOR'S NOTE

This model index consists of author and subject entries derived from single issues of 12 periodicals. A full-scale *Sex index* would cover at least three or four times as many titles on a quarterly or semiannual basis.

Since standard subject-heading schemes—like that developed by the Library of Congress—are, to put it charitably, almost *asexual*, a special thesaurus—rooted in the material itself—must necessarily be devised to fairly and usefully represent sexologic topics. BONDAGE AND DISCIPLINE, for example, while a common term in sexuality literature, doesn't even appear as a cross-reference in the LC scheme. And the same is (incredibly) true for HOMOPHOBIA, ANALINGUS, SEXUAL FANTASIES, DILDOS, SEXUAL FREEDOM, HETEROSEXUALITY, GAY RIGHTS, GAY POETS, GAY COUPLES, LESBIAN MOTHERS, SEXUAL REVOLUTION, PREMATURE EJACULATION, SEX AIDS, THREESOMES, COPROPHILIA, MATE-SWAPPING, NUDE BEACHES, SEX SHOPS, and the various fetishes. By contrast, the LC list *does* "validate" the judgmental—indeed, puritannical—descriptor, SEXUAL DEVIATION, which it unsurprisingly cross-references from "Sexual Perversion"!

Headings employed for the model:

— mainly reflect the language actually and preponderantly found in the indexed magazines, that basic vocabulary being augmented by a few primary forms and cross-references derived from sources like Erwin J. Haeberle's *Sex atlas* (Seabury Press, 1978), Bernhardt J. Hurwood's *Whole sex catalogue* (Pinnacle Books, 1975), Joan K. Marshall's *On equal terms: A Thesaurus for Non-Sexist Indexing and Cataloging* (Neal-Schuman, 1977), and the *Hennepin County Library Authority file;*

— follow "natural word order" both to ensure consistency and avoid awkward constructions like EJACULATION, PREMATURE or BEACHES, NUDE;

— represent unbiased terminology, excluding "loaded" nomenclature like "deviance," "perversion," and "pornography," but favoring self-declared group names (e.g., GAYS instead of HOMOSEXUALS);

— embody popular rather than "clinical" or "academic" terms (e.g., TEENAGERS' SEXUALITY instead of ADOLESCENT SEXUALITY) and include "slang" or "street" cross-references (e.g., from "Fucking" and "Cunt shaving") in order to promote access by the greatest possible range of users, not merely specialists or researchers.

CONTRIBUTORS

Sanford Berman is Head Cataloger at the Hennepin County Library in Edina, Minnesota. In 1971, he wrote the landmark critique *Prejudices and Antipathies: A Tract on the LC Subject Heads Concerning People* (Scarecrow Press), for six years edited the award-winning *HCL Cataloging Bulletin*, and has lately authored *The Joy of Cataloging*, an unorthodox amalgam of essays, letters, and reviews (Oryx Press, 1980).

Vern Bullough is Dean of the Faculty of Natural and Social Sciences, State University College of Buffalo, Buffalo, New York.

Richard C. Dahl is Professor and Director of the Law Library, Arizona State University, Tempe, Arizona. He is co-author of *Military Dictionary* (1960), *The American Judge: A Bibliography* (1968), and *Effective Speaking for Lawyers* (1969).

Barrett W. Elcano is Assistant Chair of the Reference Department, Oviatt Library, California State University, Northridge, California.

J. J. Gayford is a Consultant Psychiatrist at Warlingham Park Hospital in Surrey, England. He is the Consultant to the Regional Alcoholic Unit at the same hospital, and is the Consultant in charge of the Psychosexual Clinic for the Croyden Area. Dr. Gayford is also the Psychiatric Tutor at Warlingham Park Hospital and the Croydon Area, and was recently appointed Honorary Senior Lecturer at St. George's Hospital, London.

Cynthia R. Howe has a BA in English from Lawrence University and a Masters of Science in Conservation and Journalism from the University of Michigan.

Roy M. Mersky is Professor of Law and Director of the Tarlton Law Library, University of Texas at Austin.

Frederick McEnroe is a graduate student in Modern European History at San Francisco State University, a staff member of the Center for Homosexual Education, Evaluation and Research (CHEER), and Book Review and Annotated Bibliography Editor for the *Journal of Homosexuality*.

Joe Morehead is Associate Professor, School of Library and Information Science, The University at Albany, Albany, New York. He is the author of *Introduction to United States Public Documents*, 2nd ed. (Libraries Unlimited, 1978) and *Theory and Practice in Library Education: The Teaching-Learning Process* (Libraries Unlimited, 1980), as well as over 70 articles and 130 reviews and annotations, and was the first recipient of the ALA's 1977 Congressional Information Service, Documents to the People award.

Jerold Nelson is Assistant Professor in the School of Librarianship, University of Washington, Seattle, Washington, where he teaches a seminar in intellectual freedom.

Michael L. Richmond is Assistant Professor of Law and Director of Research, Nova University Law Center, Ft. Lauderdale, Florida.

Bruce A. Shuman is Associate Professor of Library and Information Studies at Queens College of the City University of New York. He has written over a dozen published articles and is completing work on a textbook of case studies in public library services, to be published shortly by The Oryx Press.

Karen Dalziel Tallman is currently employed as a Serials Librarian at the Iowa State University Library, Ames, Iowa. She is on the advisory committee for the publication *American Libraries* and has done research for contributors to several professional journals.

Lawrence S. Thompson is Professor of Classics, University of Kentucky, Lexington, Kentucky, where he has also served as University Librarian.

INDEX

Abolitionist, 78
Advocate, 88
Aeneid, 16
Agriculture Research, 70
Air University Review, 70, 72
Alciphron, 14
American Association of Sex Educators, Counselors, and Therapists (AASECT), 77
American Civil Liberties Union, 38
American Education, 71
American Social Hygiene Association, 78
Anatomy of Censorship, 33
Antologia palatina, 9
Apuleius, 3, 15
Arcadie, 78
Archives for Sexual Behavior, 76
Aristophanes, 13
Army Reserve Magazine, 71
Ars amatoria, 9
Art in antiquity, 10–12, 15
Askew, Rubin, 40
Association for Moral and Social Hygiene, 78
Augustus the Strong, 15

Band of Angels, 13
Beardsley, Aubrey, 3
Ben, Lisa, 88
Birth control, 80–81
Bizarre, 54
Black News Digest, 71
Bloch, Iwan, 77
Boys and Sex, 65
British Vigilance Association, 78
Brodsky, Joseph, 4
Bryant, Anita, 38
Bulletin Abolitioniste, 78
Bulletin Continental, 78
Business America, 71

California State University, Northridge, 76, 79
Carter, Jimmy, 37
Catcher in the Rye, 6
Censorship
  by librarians, 31, 35–36
  community standards, 3, 31–32, 54
  First Amendment, 1–2

geographical distribution, 60
incidents, 4–7, 47, 55, 57–62
language, 4
opposition tactics, 37–38, 40–41
Center for Homosexual Education, Evaluation and Research (CHEER), 79
Chardin, Teilhard de, 38
Children Today, 70
Children's reading habits, 63–64
  parental guidance, 64–66
Civil Rights Digest, 71
Civil Service Journal
  see *Management*
Collection "Guillaume Budé," 10
Colton, Helen, 7
Come Out, 89
Congressional Record, 73
Corpus vasorum, 10–11
Cosmopolitan, 53
Coyote (Come Off Your Old Tired Ethics), 79

Daily, Jay, 33
Daughters of Bilitis, 88
Deep Throat, 40
Delta Collection, 51, 54
Department of State Newsletter, 72
Dewing, Henry B., 15
Donahue, 6
Douglas, William O., 49–50

Effeminism, 85
Ellis, Havelock, 4, 77
Eros, 2
Erotica, 96–97
Evergreen Review, 55
Extension Review, 72

Fag Rag, 89
FBI Law Enforcement Bulletin, 69–70
Federal Reserve Bulletin, 72
Fear of the Word, 31
Fetish Times, 99
Flynt, Larry, 2, 11
Forum, 7, 77
Freud, Sigmund, 77
Friendship and Freedom, 87

Gaines, Ervin, 7
Gay, 89
Gay Insurgent, 99
Gay Power, 89
Gay Sunshine, 89, 99
Gays
　see Homosexuality
Gerber, Henry, 87
Gibson girls, 3
Ginzberg, Ralph, 2
Girls and Sex, 65
Good Housekeeping, 53
Guccione, Bob, 5
Guyon, Rene, 77

Haag, Ernest van den, 36
Hair, 13
Haire, Norman, 77
Harris, Frank, 3
Haworth Press, 99
Heffner, Hugh, 5
Hirschfeld, Magnus, 76-77
Homosexuality, 9, 76-77, 81-85, 87-89
　bibliography, 89-96
Horace, 10
Hrotswitha van Gandersheim, 13
Human Digest, 99
Human Sexuality, 78
Hustler, 2, 11, 54, 57, 60

Insel, 78
Institute for Sex Research, 51, 79
Intellectual freedom, 65
International Women's Year, 72

Jahrbuch fur sexuelle Zwischenstüffen, 76, 87
Janus Society Newsletter, 88
Journal of Alternate Life Styles, 78
Journal of Homosexual Counseling, 77
Journal of Homosexuality, 77, 99
Journal of Sex Education, 77
Journal of Sex Research, 76
Joyce, James, 3

Kinsey, Alfred, 77
Kittredge, George Lyman, 9
Krafft-Ebing, 69
Krauss, Friedrich S., 76
Kries, 78

Ladder, 78, 88
Lady Chatterley's Lover, 3, 40
Language, demotic, 4
Lawrence, D. H., 5, 40
Lee, Gypsy Rose, 15
Lesbian Tide, 89

Lesbians
　see Homosexuality
Leunbach, J. H., 77
Library Bill of Rights, 37, 63, 65
Library materials, destruction of, 10-11
Library of Congress
　see Delta Collection
Lindsey, Ben, 77
Liston, Robert, 32-33
Lolita, 3
Lost Cause Press, 13
Lucian, 14

Management, 71
Manpower
　see *Worklife*
Mattachine Foundation
　see Mattachine Society
Mattachine Review, 78, 88
Mattachine Society, 88
Medical Aspects of Human Sexuality, 78
Memoirs of a Woman of Pleasure, 3
Menander, 14
Mental Health Digest, 70
Meyers, Duane H., 65
Military Chaplains' Review, 72
Miller, Henry, 3
Miller vs. California, 413 U.S. 15 (1973), 47, 49-50, 55, 57
Moliere, Jean Baptiste Poquelin, 14
Monthly Labor Review, 70-71
Motif Index, 9
Ms., 55
Museo Segreto
　see Vatican Library

New Yorker, 9
Newman, Edwin, 4
Newsletter on Intellectual Freedom, 29, 57

O! Calcutta, 13
Oboler, Eli, 31
Obscene Publications Act (Great Britain), 1959, 17
Obscenity
　see Pornography
Obscenity Commission (U.S.), 1968, 64
Obscenity legislation, 47, 49-50, 55-56
Office of Intellectual Freedom, 38
Oklahoma County Libraries, 65-66
One, 53, 76, 78, 88
One Institute Library, 79
Oui, 29, 39, 41, 43-44, 46, 57
Ovid, 9

Penthouse, 1, 5, 7, 29–31, 39, 41, 43–44, 46, 48, 55, 57–58, 78
Petronius, 15
Petty girls, 3
Pillow Talk, 99
Plato, 3
Playboy, 1, 5, 7, 29–31, 33, 39, 41, 43–46, 48, 55, 57, 78
Pornography
  see also Sex magazines
  in art, 10–12, 15
  children, effect upon, 5
  definition, 2–3, 17, 31, 33, 47, 54, 57, 72
  legal proceedings, 6–7, 47, 55
  profit motive, 5
Price List 36, 71
Procopius, 15
Progressive Fish-Culturist, 70
Psychopharmacology Bulletin, 69
Psychosexuality, 17–20, 24, 85
Public Health Reports, 69

Quarterly Journal of the Library of Congress, 70

Rand, Sally, 1
Response, 99
The Right to Know: Censorship in America, 32
Rohleder, Hermann, 76
Rossi, Lee D., 31
Roth vs. United States, 354 U.S. 476, 489 (1957), 49
Russell, Bertrand, 47, 77

Sade, Marquis de, 15
Sado-masochism
  see Psychosexuality
Sappho of Lesbos, 9
Schiele, Egon, 3
Screw, 99
Selective Index to U.S. Government Periodicals, 70–71
Serial Set, 72
Sex in U.S. government publications, 69–73
Sex Information and Education Council of the United States (SIECUS), 77
Sex magazines
  advertising content, 24–25
  bibliography, 79–85, 99–135
  definition, 30
  editors, 20
  illustrations, 21, 29–31, 35
  letters to the editor, 20–21
  mailing, 49
  number of, 1, 27, 61

publishers, 20
readers, 23
social influence, 23–25, 61, 63–67
sales restrictions, 20
scholarly value, 1, 25, 75–79
subscription price, 17–18, 44
titles, 21–22
Sex magazines in the library
  cataloging, 7–8, 41–42, 49
  circulating, 42–44, 50
  indexes, 7–8, 27, 75, 99–135
  microfilm, 43–44, 49
  subscribing, 7, 30, 33–35, 38–41, 48–50
  theft of, 8, 10–11
Sex research, 79–80
Sexism, 72
Sexological Congresses, 79
Sexology, 75–79, 99
Sexual deviancy
  see Psychosexuality
Sexual Law Reporter, 77, 99
Shakespeare, William, 15, 73
SIECUS Report, 77
Social Security Bulletin, 72
Society for Human Rights, 87
Society for the Scientific Study of Sex, 76
Soldiers, 70
So's Your Old Lady, 99
Sophocles, 12
Standard Periodicals Directory, 27
Stewart, Potter, 2, 32, 63
Stonewall Inn riot, 88
Straton of Sardis, 9
A Streetcar Named Desire, 9
Suetonius, 11

Thompson, Lawrence S., 9
Townsend, William H., 13
Transvestism
  see Psychosexuality
Tropic of Cancer, 3
Tropic of Capricorn, 3

Ulrichs, Karl Heinrich, 87
Ulysses, 3
Ustinov, Peter, 4–5

Vancouver Sun, 1
Variations, 99
Vatican Library, 7, 11
Vice Versa, 78, 88
Vector, 88
Vergil, 16
Vierteljahrsberichte des wissenschaftlich-humanitären Komitees, 76
Vriendschap, 78

Warren, Robert Penn, 13
Weg, 78
H. W. Wilson Company, 99
Women and Work, 71
Worklife, 72
World League for Sexual Reform, 76–77

Zeitschrift für Sexualwissenschaft, 76

For Product Safety Concerns and Information please contact our EU
representative GPSR@taylorandfrancis.com
Taylor & Francis Verlag GmbH, Kaufingerstraße 24, 80331 München, Germany

www.ingramcontent.com/pod-product-compliance
Lightning Source LLC
Chambersburg PA
CBHW052129300426
44116CB00010B/1836